D1148089

THE
WINE
DRINKERS
ALMANAC

Don Philpott

LOCHAR PUBLISHING · MOFFAT · SCOTLAND

© Don Philpott, 1991

Published by Lochar Publishing Ltd
Moffat DG10 9ED

British Library Cataloguing in Publication Data
Philpott, Don
    The Wine Drinkers' Almanac.
    1. Wines
    I. Title
    641.22

ISBN 0-948403-79-9

Typeset in 9 on 10pt Garamond 49 by
Chapterhouse, Formby

Printed in Scotland by Eagle Colour Books Ltd

Contents

Acknowledgements

The author would like to thank Helena Harwood,
Executive Secretary of the Wine Promotion Board
and David Gill M.W. for all their help and advice, as
well as other friends in the wine trade the world over,
for their assistance and support.

Introduction

Many wine drinkers would like to be more
adventurous but are reluctant to experiment by
choosing an unknown wine which may disappoint.
The trouble is that there is so much wine on offer.
Wine drinkers have never had such choice. There are
literally tens of thousands of wines and scores of
countries around the globe producing them.
The aim of this book is to provide the information
needed so that people will feel encouraged to
experiment.
The Wine Drinkers' Almanac is unique in that it
provides three easy ways of discovering hundreds of
wines which should be to your liking.
All the major wine-producing countries are included
with clear descriptions covering the style and
character of the wines produced.
When specific grape varieties are used, details are
given so that if you like a particular wine, you can
find out which one produced it, and then look for
other wines around the world made from the same
variety.
Thirdly, every wine listed in the Almanac has been
given a number or letter symbol. This coding system
has been created by the UK Wine Promotion Board
and provides an at-a-glance reference to allow you to
choose wines of a similar style worldwide.
So, if you have a favourite wine, you should now be
able to choose hundreds of others like it by selecting
those made from either the same grape variety, or
those produced with the same style and taste.

Don Philpott

Using the red and white wine taste guides

Have you ever wondered whether you'd enjoy a red wine you've never tasted before? Have you ever bought a white wine new to you and found it a little too dry, or too sweet?

Of course, white wines have more characteristics than dryness or sweetness – but many people find their enjoyment of a particular white wine is largely dependent on this aspect.

Similarly with red wines, how do you go about selecting a wine that matches the fullness of flavour you would ideally like for the occasion?

The Wine Promotion Board, an independent UK body, has produced two easy-to-use wine taste guides, one for white wines and the other for reds. Both are now widely used throughout Britain.

The white wine guide covers all the major white wines of the world, as well as rosé, sherry and vermouth, by using a scale of sweetness numbered 1 to 9. The lower the number the dryer the wine, so number 1 signifies very dry wines like Chablis and Muscadet, while number 9 indicates maximum sweetness, in wines such as Malmsey Madeira and Trockenbeerenauslese. The numbers in between span the remaining dryness-to-sweetness spectrum, helping consumers identify the white wines they are likely to enjoy best.

The red wine guide works in a slightly different way, using five categories from A to E. These categories identify styles of red wine in terms of total taste – in other words, the impression they give to the palate. They start at A with wines comparable to Beaujolais or light German reds, and equally enjoyable with or without food. At E, the other end of the scale, are the bigger and more concentrated styles with a greater sensation of depth and fullness. These wines, like Shiraz from Australia and Barolo from Italy, are often more suitable for drinking with food.

The world of wine is very complex and there can be variations due to wine making techniques, from the taste suggestions in the guide. Hungarian Tokay, for instance, comes in varying degrees of sweetness, while the more expensive fine wines – those which go on maturing in the bottle – change in complexity and cannot adequately be covered by the taste guide. The vast majority of wines, however, do fit happily into one or other of the taste guide categories, and you should be able to find the ones to suit you by playing the 'letters and numbers' game in the following pages.

White wine guide code

1. Bergerac
   Blanquette de
     Limoux
   Champagne
     (dry)
   Chablis
   Dry white
     Bordeaux
   Entre-Deux-Mers

   Manzanilla
     Sherry
   Muscadet
   Pouilly Fumé
   Sancerre
   Saumur
   Sauvignon Blanc

   Tavel Rosé
   Touraine

2. Alella
   Chardonnay
     (from all
     countries)
   Dry English wine
   Dry Montilla
   Dry Sherry
   Dry sparkling
     wine (Brut)
   Fendant
   Fino Sherry

   Frascati Secco
   German Trocken
     wines
   Graves
   La Mancha
   Navarra
   Orvieto Secco
   Pale Dry Cyprus
     Sherry
   Penedès
   Provence Rosé

   Riesling d'Alsace
   Rueda
   Sercial Madeira
   Spanish dry
   Soave
   Valencia
   Verdicchio
   Vin de Pays
   White Burgundy
   White Rioja
   White Rhône

3. Brut Sparkling
     wine
   California
     Chardonnay
   California White
     (Blush)
     Zinfandel
   Cava sparkling
     wine
   Dry Amontillado
     Sherry
   Dry white
     Vermouth

   Grüner Veltliner
   Halbtrocken
     wines
   Hungarian dry
     Welschriesling
   Medium dry
     English
   Medium dry
     Montilla
   Medium dry
     Vermouth

   Moseltaler
   Muscat d'Alsace
   Pinot Blanc
     d'Alsace
   Sekt sparkling
     wine

4. Anjou Rosé   Hungarian Olasz
    Australian   Riesling
      Riesling   Medium dry
    Bulgarian   Sherry
      Welschriesling   New Zealand
    Chenin Blanc   Riesling
    Full Amontil-   Orvieto
      lado   Abbocato
    German   Piesporter
      Kabinett   Michelsberg
    German Quality   Portugese Rosé
      Wine Qba   Vinho Verdé
    Gewürztraminer   Yugoslav Laski
      d'Alsace   Riesling

5. Austrian   Liebfraumilch
      Spätlese   Medium Cyprus
    Dry White Port   Sherry
    EEC Table Wine   Verdelho
    Lambrusco   Madeira
      Bianco   Vouvray Demi-
                            Sec

6. Golden Sherry
    Demi-Sec Champagne and Demi-Sec sparkling wines
    German Spätlese
    Tokay Szamorodni sweet

7. Asti Spumante   German Auslese   Premières Côtes
    Bianco, Rosé and Monbazillac   de Bordeaux
      Rosso   Montilla Cream   Tokay Aszú
    Vermouth   Pale Cream   White Port
    Bual Madeira   Sherry

8. Barsac   Dark Cream/rich   Moscatels/Musc-
    Cream Cyprus   cream Sherry   ats
      Sherry   German/   Sauternes
    Cream Sherry   Austrian   Spanish sweet
                        Beerenauslese   wine

9. Brown Sherry   Malmsey   Muscat de
    German/   Madeira   Beaumes de
    Austrian   Marsala   Venise
    Trockenbeeren-
      auslese
    Malaga

Red Wine Guide Code

A. Bardolino   German red   Vin de Table
Beaujolais   wine   Vino da Tavola
EEC Table Wine   Lambrusco
Rosso
Touraine

B. Beaujolais   Navarra   Saumur
Villages and   Pinot Noir   Valdepenas
Crus   Pinotage   Valencia
Chinon   Red Burgundy
Côte de Beaune
Côtes du
Roussillon
Côtes du
Ventoux
Merlot

C. Bergerac   Corbieres
Bordeaux Rouge   Côtes du Rhône
Bulgarian   Minervois
Cabernet   North Africa
Californian   Rioja
Cabernet
Claret

D. Bairrada   Fitou   Syrah
Cabernet   Hungarian Red   Zinfandel
Sauvignon   Médoc
(not Bulgaria   Penedès
or California)   Ribera del
Châteauneuf-   Duero
du-Pape   Rioja Reservas
Chianti   Ruby and Tawny
Crozes-   Port
Hermitage
Dao

E. Barolo   Recioto della
Cyprus Red   Valpolicella
Greek Red   Shiraz (Australia
Jumilla   or South
Africa)

Making wine

Wine is the product of fermenting the juice of crushed grapes using yeast and natural grape sugar to produce alcohol. When the required level of alcohol or sweetness has been achieved, the process is stopped and the wine is put into barrels or tanks for storage or bottling.

That is all there is to it but from your own tasting you will know that some wines can be magnificent and others quite foul. The skill in wine-making is knowing how to make the best possible wine from the grapes.

The work of producing good wines starts in the vineyard. The soil and climate can influence the style of the variety planted, but many other factors come into play. How the grapes are pruned and trained on the trellises, how much water and sun the vines receive, how much spraying is done to combat pests and diseases, and how many bunches of grapes are allowed to mature on each vine all contribute to the quality of the grapes at picking, an essential prerequisite to good wine.

The point at which the grapes are picked is equally critical. If you are looking for maximum natural sugar content, as in the finest sweet German wines, you pick as late as possible. If you want high acidity, as in many of the Loire whites, you pick early or plant the vines in areas which get less sunshine. In South Africa, and now many other countries, the grapes are picked at night when it is cooler and the fruit fresher, with more trapped flavour.

The speed and method of the grapes' delivery to the winery is also important. In some countries, where the grapes have to be delivered to central wineries, it is not unusual to see lorries queueing in the blazing sunshine for many hours before they can dump their loads. By the time the lorries unload, the juice has started to ferment and the finished product will be dreadful. The best wines are often produced from grapes which are picked in small quantities into small containers and handled carefully.

Wineries can vary enormously from country to country. In peasant areas of France, Italy and Spain many wineries have changed little in decades and neither have the wine-making techniques. In California and Australia you can see some of the most modern wineries in the world. The huge investment that a modern winery involves does not automatically mean it will produce good wines. It does, however, iron out many of the problems and allows more control over the wine making process, so fewer bad wines should be made.

In the end it comes down to the skill of the wine-maker and, as many of the finest wines from the Rhône and southern Italy prove, you don't have to have the latest hi-tech wineries to produce some of the world's greatest wines.

When the grapes reach the winery the juice is extracted by putting them into a press, which also separates out the skin, pips, stalks and any stem. Almost all grape juice is clear, and red wine is coloured by allowing the juice to stay in contact with the skins. It also absorbs tannin from the stalks and pips, which gives the wine longer life. The longer the juice or 'must' remains in contact with the skins, the darker the wine will be.

For white wine, there is no need for skin contact, so the grapes are usually de-stalked on arrival at the winery and a special press used to extract the juice. Big, powerful whites are allowed some skin contact not to gain colour, but to acquire body.

A horizontal press is normally used for white wines. The grapes are put into the cylindrical container until it is full, and it then revolves. As it rotates, chains inside the container thrash the grapes and the juice runs off either to fermenting vats or barrels. A second type of horizontal press contains a central bag which is gradually inflated once the grapes have been loaded. The expanding bag pushes the grapes against the side of the container and the juice is pressed out. The amount of juice extracted is carefully controlled by the winemaker. The first pressing is generally considered to make the best wine, but wineries can go on to second and third pressings.

Usually different grape varieties are pressed
separately and the must kept apart to see how it
develops before blending takes place. In big wineries
where there is volume production, everything often
goes into the press at the same time. There is a red
Burgundy called Passe-Tout-Grain, which means
'processed all at the same time'.

Red wine and rosé get their colour from skin contact,
though a rosé obviously spends less time in contact
than a red. The slightest contact is enough to give
the wine a faintly pinkish hue.

Once the juice has been extracted and has spent its
time in contact with the skin, it is piped into
fermentation vats, where it begins its conversion into
wine.

Wine is produced when yeast, naturally occurring or
added, attacks the sugar in the grape juice, breaking
it down to release energy in the form of heat. The
action of yeast on sugar produces a number of by-
products which include carbon dioxide and, most
important of all, alcohol.

The yeast goes on working until it has used up all the
sugar in the juice, until the alcohol reaches a level
above which it cannot function, or until the
fermentation is stopped artificially. Yeasts can only
operate within certain temperature levels. If the
temperature falls they go into a state of suspension;
if the temperature rises too high, they are killed.

In the past, because of temperature fluctuations, the
aim was to complete the fermentation process as
quickly as possible, but this often led to high
temperatures and the juice being 'baked'.

Much of the massive investment in modern wineries
goes into fermentation tanks which can be
temperature-controlled. White wine particularly
benefits from slower fermentation at cooler
temperatures, because it brings out much more
flavour.

After fermentation, the white wine is usually
allowed to settle for a few days and then is filtered.
The new horizontal presses are very efficient at
extracting juice but they also allow small particles of
skin to enter the must. This is one reason why young
fermented wine has such a cloudy, milky

appearance, and the particules must be removed.
At this stage the wine-maker can 'adjust' the wine.
In many countries sugar can be added, a process
called chaptalisation. This reduces the acidity of the
wine. In many regulated areas sugar is not allowed,
and the wine-makers have to use concentrated must,
which raises both the alcohol content and the acidity
levels. The wine-maker may also add small
quantities of chalk to reduce acidity if necessary.
Concrete vats and stainless steel tanks have taken
over from the traditional oak barrels in many places.
The barrels may look fine in a cellar but they are
generally not as efficient as the modern storage
containers. Stainless steel tanks have the added
advantage that they can be used for fermenting,
storage and blending, while wood is difficult to clean
and hugely expensive.
Only occasionally is white wine allowed to ferment a
second time – a process called malolactic
fermentation – to reduce acidity levels. This
technique is still used in parts of Chablis and the
Loire, for instance. It usually happens in the spring
when the warmer weather stimulates dormant yeasts.
If the wine is not to have secondary fermentation, it
must be removed from the vats, and this process is
known as racking or back blending. Before this can
happen the wine-maker must decide the style of
wine he wants. If it is to be medium or sweet, the
fermentation will have to be stopped artificially
using filters. The wine is passed through very fine
screens which extract all the yeast so there can be no
more fermentation. In some areas, Germany for
example, sweet natural juice is then added to
increase the residual sugar content of the wine.
The wine is drawn off the lees (the sediment at the
bottom of the fermentation tanks) using filters or a
centrifuge. Next, the wine is stabilised to prevent the
formation of tartaric acid crystals, a harmless
substance which occurs naturally in wine but which
must cause more complaints to wine waiters than
anything else. To prevent these crystals forming, the
wine is cooled to about -5C and held in this state for
several days before its final bottling, labelling and
dispatch.

The red wine-making method is different from the beginning. In Burgundy, for instance, the stems are often kept on for pressing, while in Bordeaux they are rarely used. During fermentation of red wines, the skins, stems and so on float to the surface of the vats. This 'cap' is vulnerable to attack from bacteria which would taint the wine, so in traditional wineries, men are employed with long poles to keep it mixed. In modern wineries, fermenting juice is sucked up and showered over the surface at regular intervals to prevent the cap forming.

After fermentation, most of the wine is run off. There is still a lot of wine trapped in the pulp of stems, etc, and this is known as the 'marc'. It has to be pressed again to release extra juices which are held separately.

The first press from the marc can produce good quality wine, but subsequent pressings are usually destined for distillation.

The wine is 'fined' and filtered to extract any remaining solids, and is then piped into barrels or tanks. Most red wine undergoes secondary fermentation during this stage.

As the wine develops, it is up to the wine-maker to decide whether to make varietal wines (only one grape variety allowed) or a blend. If the wine is not to be aged for long periods, it may be pasteurised to sterilise it before bottling. If it is to be aged, it will usually go deep into the vineyard's cellars and be kept in oak barrels, the size of which varies depending on the country, or even the region. Wine can age in the bottle as well, and many of the world's finest wines are those which have a combination of both barrel and bottle ageing.

Buying wine

The choice of wine available to the consumer has never been greater and nor have the methods of buying it. One of the most pleasurable ways to buy wine is to visit the growers' cellars and taste before you make your decision. For wines from further afield, there are specialist shippers, merchants and wine shops which can introduce you to the wines of the world. Tastings are becoming much more common in retail wine outlets, especially wine warehouses where you buy by the case.

All merchants and wine stores will negotiate special deals for large orders, so it is always worth buying with a group of friends to get the maximum discounts, or you could consider setting up your own wine club.

Most people buy their wine through normal retail outlets or wine clubs, but auctions can yield some great bargains and they are not as imposing as you might think – so long as you exercise self-discipline! Many leading French producers and a growing number of others offer a proportion of their wine for sale shortly after the vintage each year. This wine is sold '*en primeur*' and the producers use it to test demand. If there is a rush to buy, the price usually goes up, so buying early can save you money.

Buying *en primeur*, however, can have pitfalls. It is not unknown for prices to come down and you have to be able to tell how the very young wine will develop in perhaps five or ten years' time.

I think the *en primeur* gamble is worthwhile. Don't opt for the *premier cru* wines or top *domaines* but go for wines that you know you like, and which you will enjoy drinking when they are mature.

If you choose wisely, buying wines in this way can be a very good drinking investment. Some of the best growths in Bordeaux can increase in price tenfold over a decade and there are similar benefits in choosing the best wines from Germany or California. Making that extra investment and buying two cases of the best wines instead of one means you can enjoy the first dozen and sell the second at a profit.

Storing wine

If you are buying wine to lay down, the problem is where to keep it. Having made the investment it is essential to store the wine properly until it is ready for drinking. The ideal store is the old-fashioned cellar, where the air temperature is constant, the humidity is not too high and there is a reasonable flow of air. Modern architecture, however, means few of us have this luxury.

The main requirement in choosing storage space is finding a place where the temperature does not fluctuate. Wine can withstand cold but it cannot cope with constantly changing temperatures. There is a lot of nonsense talked about correct temperatures, but obviously a storage spot next to the hot water boiler is not suitable, nor is a space in the attic, where the sun's heat can raise the temperature by many degrees each day, before it plunges back down during the night.

It is usually possible, however, to find somewhere in the home where wine can be stored correctly. A cupboard under the stairs or in an unheated spare bedroom may be suitable. You can use insulating materials such as foam blocks or polystyrene, and there are even commercial cabinets, electrically cooled to ensure the wine is kept at the right temperatures so that it ages slowly and correctly.

If you are storing a lot of wine, it is worth the effort to prepare a special room for it. You could convert part of the roof space using insulating materials so that the temperature is constant and the humidity about 65 per cent. Maintaining an air flow is essential to prevent mould on the bottles and condensation. Damp will also cause labels to come off, which may cause confusion.

Wine must always be stored on its side so that the corks stay moist. If the cork dries out, it shrinks and air enters the bottle. The wine becomes oxidised and you finish up with expensive vinegar.

Wines don't like to be disturbed so they should be moved as little as possible. You should never contemplate drinking a really fine old wine until several weeks after buying it because it needs time to settle. And great care must be taken when you fetch it from its storage space into the dining room.

If you are planning a dinner party you should collect the wines from their storage space at least 12 hours (ideally a day) before they are needed. This allows them to warm up to room temperature and allows any sediment to settle. The practice of some top restaurants of bringing the red wine up to room temperature by popping it in the microwave for a few seconds is not to be encouraged.

Most wines do not require decanting and the corks can be pulled about 30 minutes before they are needed. Red wines do improve if they are allowed to breathe, and fine old reds should be handled with great care.

Decanting

The aim of decanting is to remove the sediment from old wine and some ports so that the diner is not offered cloudy wine. Decanting requires a steady hand and a good eye and is best performed in private.

When decanting, light a candle and position it so that the flame illuminates the neck of the bottle. Then disgorge the wine via a funnel into the decanter. Keep the base of the bottle as low as possible and keep your eye on the neck. You should be able to spot the sediment as it slowly rises in the bottle. The aim is to stop pouring before any escapes. Decanting invariably means leaving some wine in the bottle, but the wine in the decanter should be clear and, hopefully, wonderful.

Many fine old Bordeaux and Burgundy wines benefit from decanting, but it is a subject of fierce debate. In Burgundy it is very unusual to decant old bottles but doing so is easy and can maximise drinking pleasure. Vintage port also needs decanting, and many other fine old reds from other countries can also benefit from this practice. One added bonus is that a good glass or crystal decanter looks splendid on the dining table.

Serving wine

Good wine deserves good glass. Crystal is fine but it can interfere with your perception and appreciation of the colour of the wine. I prefer clean, clear and large glasses. Clean glasses are essential because there is almost nothing worse than being offered wine in a glass which reeks of washing-up liquid.

Nor is it pleasing to be given wine in a small glass. This is not just a matter of greed, but because wine needs to breathe and you must be able to appreciate the *bouquet* given off. A large glass should be used and only half-filled, so there is space between the surface of the wine and the rim of the glass, where the aromas can gather.

Using large glasses also makes life much easier if you are the host, because you don't have to go round filling them up so often.

There is also much argument about the correct serving temperature for different wines. As a general rule, lighter-style reds often benefit from slight chilling while big, gutsy reds drink better just a little above room temperature. An extra degree or two can soften any rough edges the wine may have. Everyday Bordeaux should be drunk at room temperature while older clarets should be drunk just a little cooler and red Burgundy-style wines cooler still. Most whites and rosés should be served well chilled, as should non-vintage Champagne and most other sparkling wines. That means an hour or two in the fridge and then the wine should be kept cool in an ice bucket or similar cooling device.

Fine white Burgundies and the better full-bodied whites from other parts of the world – Australian and Californian Chardonnay for instance – Champagne and similar classy, sparkling wines require less chilling and should only be put in the fridge for thirty minutes or so. These big, full-bodied whites then have the chance to warm up in the glass, releasing their bouquets.

It may be heresy, but if guests do arrive unexpectedly and you need to cool white or sparkling wine in a

hurry, put it in the freezer for 10–15 minutes.
Some Sherry, Madeira, Port and other fortified wines
also benefit from being served chilled. Fino Sherry
and Manzanilla should be served well chilled and
white port is best served cold.

When it comes down to it, however, as with all
matters concerning wine, do what you prefer. After
all, what matters most is that you enjoy it.

Algeria

History: The wine-making tradition is more than 2,000 years old and wine was exported to Rome for the courts of the Caesars. Moslem domination ended wine production but grapes were still grown as fresh fruit and for raisins.

Current situation: Modern wine production started about 130 years ago with the first French settlers and the first vineyards were planted in 165. As French vineyards were decimated by phylloxera, many growers moved to Algeria to start again, bringing with them their own regional varieties. Thirty years ago, Algeria was one of the world's leading wine producers. Algeria was still a French territory until 1962, and had more than 900,000 acres of vines and produced 1,500 million litres of wine. The vineyards area has since halved and the government wants annual production pegged at around 300 million litres a year. Red accounts for about two-thirds of production and most is sole in bulk. Whites and rosés have improved considerably although quality varies enormously.

Classification: The classification system is largely based on the French, with VDQS and Appellation d'Origine Garantie. In reality it means little.

Grapes: Grape varieties planted usually reflected the region of France the settlers came from. People from Burgundy planted Pinot Noir and Gamay, those from Bordeaux introduced the Cabernet varieties, and those from the south Grenache, Mourvèdre and so on.
The main varieties today are: Red – Cabernet Sauvignon, Carignan, Cinsault, Grenache, Pinot Noir, Morastel, Mourvèdre, Syrah; White – Clairette, Muscat.

Regions: Vineyards are found in the three coastal Departments of Oran, Alger and Constantine. Most of the wine is grown on the plains but the best results come from the hillside vineyards in the south of Oran and Alger.

Oran: Designated areas are: Coteaux de Mascara (produces the best reds), Coteaux de Tlemcen (the best whites), Monts du Tessalah, Mostaganem, Mostaganem-Kenenda, Oued-Imbert.

Alger: Designated areas are: Ain-Bessem-Bouira, Coteaux du Zaccar, Haut-Dahra, Medea.

Styles: *Reds*: Big, strong, heady, earthy wines. Drink youngish, but best will age.
Whites: Much improved. Best are fresh, crisp, aromatic with good fruit. Drink young.
Rosés: Fresh, fruity, quaffable. Must be drunk very young.

HUMBERTO CANALE

VINO FINO TINTO
de RIO NEGRO
Vintage 1985

Humberto Canale

Fine Red Wine

Produced and Bottled by
Est. H. CANALE S.A.
Chacra 186 - Gral. Roca   I.N.V.R.N. 105.992
Bodega N. 70695   Embotellado en Origen

ALCOHOL 12,50% BY VOL   PRODUCT OF ARGENTINA   NET CONTENTS 750 ml
ESTATE GROWN & BOTTLED

Argentina

History: The first vineyard was planted in 1556 by Father Cedron, a Jesuit priest. He planted a variety called Criolla and there are at least five related strains still grown for everyday, uninteresting white, red and rosé. The first Italian and French settlers arrived about 100 years ago and, using water from the Andes for irrigation, they transformed Mendoza province from a near-desert into a fertile area of vineyards.

Current situation: The world's fifth largest wine producer, with about 850,000 acres of vineyards producing about 4,000 million litres of wine and enormous potential. Classic varieties have started to replace traditional varieties with very promising results. Very hot summers and plentiful irrigation provides huge yields, and quality will be improved when quantity is reduced, and wineries are modernised.
The best local variety is Torrontes for whites. The best whites are crisp and fresh, the best reds have

good fruit but this is often lost because of over-ageing in oak. New-style wines with more flavour and varietal characteristics are emerging.

Classification: There is no classification system, but labels usually indicate the variety and region of origin. The size of the country and distance between wine regions usually makes blending from other areas impractical.

Grapes: The main local red grape is Criolla Grande, which is used to produce big, fruity reds for the home market. The wines spend too much time in large, oak barrels where they lose flavour and become dominated by oak. Main imported grape varieties are Malbec, Cabernet Sauvignon, Riesling, Chardonnay, Sémillon, Chenin Blanc and Sauvignon Blanc.

Regions: *Mendoza*: The largest wine region, in the shadows of the Andes, with more than two-thirds of the country's vineyards. Mostly red wines from Malbec and Cabernet Sauvignon, which produces the best wine if not aged too long.

San Juan and La Rioja: In the north and very hot, producing mostly whites which are high in alcohol and low in acidity. Also produces heady fortified and dessert wines and some sparkling wines.

Rio Negro: A southern region with great potential but, as yet, few vineyards. Plantings of Cabernet Sauvignon, Merlot and Sémillon.

Catamarca: A small region north of San Juan, mostly producing grapes for brandy.

Salta: Cool mountain vineyards in the far north. Vineyard acreage is increasing and whites, especially Torrontes, have good potential.

Other promising areas: Cordoba, Entre Ríos, Lictoral, Occidente and Norte.

Styles: *Reds*: *Malbec* (C) can be light, spicy and fruity, but becomes dull and loses fruit if aged too long. Best drunk young. The best *Cabernet Sauvignon* (D) rich, plummy, fruit. Will age.

Whites: *Chardonnay* (2) is rich, creamy and wood-edged, with complex fruit. Drink youngish.

Torrontes (2) – a local white variety, is aromatic, flowery and fragrant with a hint of sweetness; similar to a dry Muscat. Drink youngish.

SOUTH EASTERN AUSTRALIA
DRY WHITE WINE

1988

PRODUCED AND BOTTLED BY TOLLANA WINES
TANUNDA ROAD NURIOOTPA SOUTH AUSTRALIA 5355
EXPORTED BY OMEGA WINES LTD CANTERBURY KENT CT4 5LH

750ml WINE MADE IN AUSTRALIA 10.5% VOL

Australia

History: The Australian wine industry is more than
200 years old. Vines were planted by the first settlers
who sailed with Captain Arthur Phillips's fleet of
eleven ships. They landed at what is now the Sydney
suburbs in 1788 and the first vineyard was on a site
now occupied by Sydney's Botanical Gardens. The
area was too humid, the vines died from disease and
the search started for more favourable sites. New
vineyards were planted inland on the Paramatta and
the Australian wine industry was born. For the best
part of 100 years, exports were tailored to the British
market and consisted largely of beefy 'Burgundy-
style' reds, and cheap fortified wines.

Current situation: Australia has some of the finest
vineyards in the world but the search for new and
better sites continues relentlessly. Growers are
moving further inland and establishing new
vineyards at altitude. Australia has been one of the
wine world's success stories of the last decade. It has

produced world-beating, gloriously uninhibited, economical wines and notched up remarkable exports, especially in Britain. In the early 1960s, wine drinking at home began to rival beer consumption and producers started a massive replanting programme in an attempt to cope with the demand for whites. Since then, the industry has never looked back.

Vines are grown in every state and in virtually every type of terrain, including the sun-baked desert of Alice Springs deep in the Northern Territories, although this is more of a curiosity than a serious contender for a Gold Medal.

A major reason for the industry's success is that it has not been constrained by the strict traditions followed in Europe. Vine growers and wine-makers have been able to experiment and in the process have discovered new techniques which are now being copied in wineries worldwide. The final element in the success story is the winery. Faced with massive consumer demand in the 1960s, the wineries invested heavily in new technology which saw huge leaps in quality.

The search for new and better techniques continues
relentlessly. There are experimental vineyards, new
pruning and training methods, and while wine-
makers have always been anxious to produce 'clean'
wines, the emphasis is now very much on flavour,
and this is the keynote of Australian wines. Today
there are more than 600 producers with about
135,000 acres of vines in Australia, yielding around
400 million litres a year (a record 495 million litres in
1989). Fewer than ten companies, however, account
for almost 90 per cent of total production.

Classification: There is no national classification
system but quality controls have been introduced in
a number of areas – Margaret River, Mudgee, Hunter
Valley, Tasmania, Victoria and Queensland's
Granite Belt. Generally, quality is assessed by the
wine's success in the many national wine shows. The
number of Gold and other medals won is usually
indicated on the back label.

Grapes: Australia's fine wine reputation has been
built on a handful of grape varieties. Principal red
varieties are Shiraz (Syrah in France), Cabernet
Sauvignon, Granache and increasingly Pinot Noir,
which is often a fabulous performer.
The main white varieties are Muscat, Riesling,
Marsanne, Sémillon and Sauvignon Blanc. The
acreage of Chardonnay has quadrupled in recent
years as worldwide demand forces up grape prices.
Now Australia has so much Chardonnay that the
grape price has fallen, which means lots of great
value wine.
Under Australian wine law, varietals can contain up
to 20 per cent of another grape variety. A lot of
Australian wine is blended and even varietals often
use wine of the same variety from other regions.

Regions and Styles

NEW SOUTH WALES
The oldest wine-producing region with about 23,000
acres of vines yielding about 100 million litres of
wine.

Canberra: Traditional wine area rediscovered in 1971. Now it contains a dozen small wineries producing cool-climate whites and reds which bring out full fruit flavour. Almost all the wine is sold locally.

Lower Hunter Valley: Producing wine since 1820s, and noted for its red volcanic soil which helps produce some stunning whites and gusty reds. Hunter Valley Sémillon (2) ages wonderfully in the bottle. Although not aged in wood it develops toasted oak flavours, honeyed richness. New-style wines are buttery rich and made to be drunk young. Hunter Valley Shiraz (D) has an intense deep colour, is big and beefy, and gives off sweaty leather aromas when aged. New-style is for richer, fruitier, spicy flavours.

Mudgee: The wine-makers taste each others' wines blind to determine which qualify for the Mudgee Appellation of Origin. The region produces big, plummy Cabernet Sauvignon and Shiraz wines which age well (C/D) and soft, rich, full fruit Chardonnays (2).

Murrumbidgee Irrigation Area (also known as ***Riverina***): A huge oasis in the middle of the outback, full of paddy fields, orchards and vineyards. Produces a fifth of Australia's grape harvest, much of it for bulk production. The area does, however, produce some wonderful whites such as luscious Semillon Sauternes (8) which will keep for decades, and late-harvested Rhine Rieslings (6/8). Chardonnay is showing great promise (2).

Upper Hunter Valley: Not really developed until the 1970s because of the hot, dry climate. Vines have to be drip-irrigated but produce massive yields. Produces good rich Chardonnay (2) which will age and Semillon, best drunk young (2). Cabernet Sauvignon and Pinot Noir show great promise.

VICTORIA

About 6,500 acreas of vineyards producing about 53 million litres annually. Produces wines of all styles and noted for its small, independent wineries which concentrate on quality.

Ballarat: About 75 miles north west of Melbourne, produces good sparkling wines.

Bendigo: Replanted in 1969 and noted for its eucalyptus-tasting reds. Good Cabernet Sauvignon (D) and Shiraz (D), which both age well, and promising Chardonnay (2).

Geelong: An area south of Ballarat, producing wonderful reds, especially Cabernet Sauvignon (D) bursting with fruit.

Glenrowan: Also known as Milawa and famous for its big rich, reds and luscious dessert wines. Best wines are Cabernet Sauvignon (D), Shiraz (D), and the Liqueur Muscats (8).

Goulburn Valley: The vineyards of Chateau Tahbilk were planted in 1860 and only relatively recently have other producers move in. Famous for Cabernet Sauvignon (D) and Sauvignon/Shiraz blends (D), Chardonnay (2) and Rhine Riesling (4) and wood-aged Marsanne, a big, rich white. The Valley is home to more than half the world's planting of Marsanne.

Great Western: An old wine-producing area now noted for its sparklers and its reds. Soft, velvety fruit Shiraz with hints of plain chocolate (D).

Macedon: Close to Melbourne and producing good Chardonnay (2), Rhine Riesling (4) and Cabernet Sauvignon (D).

Milawa: See *Glenrowan*.

Mornington Peninsula: South of Melbourne and famous for Shiraz (5), which is big, rich, spicy and fruity, and long-lasting (D). Also produces other quality white and reds.

Murray River: Sandwiched between Rutherglen and Riverland, a salty area of irrigated vineyards producing good whites – Chardonnay (2) and Sauvignon Blanc (1).

Pyrenees: The famous blue mountains about 120 miles north west of Melbourne. Produces very dry, minty Cabernet Sauvignon (D) and Shiraz (E), classy Chardonnay (2) and Rhine Riesling (3) and good sparkling wines.

Rutherglen: In the north-east of the state and famous for fortified wines, the best being the Liqueur Muscats and Tokays, Australia's finest (7/8). Showing great promise with table wines, especially Sémillon (2) and Gewürztraminer (4), Cabernet Sauvignon (D) and big, chunky Durif (E).

Sunraysia: Another name for the sub-region of the Murray River which includes Mildura.

Yarra Valley: About 20 miles east of Melbourne, where the first vineyards were planted by Swiss immigrants. Only Tasmania has a cooler climate but the Yarra Valley produces some great wines, especially Cabernet Sauvignon (D), Pinot Noir (B) and Cabernet/Merlot blends (B). Tremendous aromatic Gewürztraminer (4) and crisp, steely-dry, classy Rhine Riesling (2).

SOUTH AUSTRALIA
The largest vineyard state with about 70,000 acres of vines and an annual production of more than 225 million litres, about 60 per cent of Australia's total.

Adelaide Hills: A rich, hilly area east of Adelaide, producing high-quality Chardonnay (2), Rhine Riesling (2) and Cabernet Sauvignon (D). Also noted for its sparkling wine.

Adelaide Plains: A vineyard area slowly being swallowed up by Adelaide's suburban sprawl. Once the home of the fabulous Grange Hermitage, the area still produces good Cabernet Sauvignon (D).

Barossa Valley: Southern Australia's top wine-growing area: hot, dry and at altitude. Produces classy, super-crisp Rhine Riesling (2), big solid Grenache (D) and Shiraz (E), and excellent blends.

Clare Valley: The most northerly vineyards in Southern Australia, producing excellent, delicate, spicy Rhine Riesling (3), often Botrytis-affected for added richness. Also produces good Sémillon (2), Chardonnay (2) and Cabernet Sauvignon (D).

Coonawarra: The most southerly vineyards in the state, named after the Aborigine word for wild honeysuckle. Vineyards planted on terra rose over limestone, which produces wonderful Cabernet Sauvignon (D), soft, rich, perfumed and fruity, with hints of eucalyptus, and big, rich, peppery Shiraz (E). The cool temperatures also favour whites such as Chardonnay (2), rich, buttery, oaky and great value.

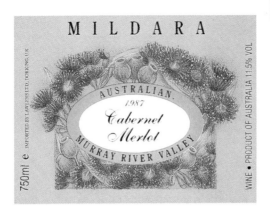

Langhorne Creek: About 50 miles south-east of Adelaide, and noted for big, beefy reds and dessert wines.

McLaren Vale: Just south of Adelaide, where the cool climate helps produce full-flavoured reds, and crisp, fresh whites. Best reds are big Cabernet Sauvignons (D) and Shiraz (E), best whites: Chardonnay (2), Rhine Riesling (2), Sémillon (2) and Sauvignon Blanc (2). Also noted for dessert wines.

Padthaway: Really part of Coonawarra but producing high quality Chardonnay, Rhine Riesling and Sauvignon Blanc (all 2).

Riverland: An extension of Victoria's Murray River, producing mostly cask wines, but fine Rhine Riesling (2), Chardonnay (2), Sauvignon Blanc (2), and in the reds, Cabernet Sauvignon (D) Cabernet/Melbec (C) and Shiraz (E).

Watervale: Part of the Clare but prized for its Shiraz (E) and Cabernet Sauvignon (D).

WESTERN AUSTRALIA

The smallest vineyard state, with about 5,000 acres and an annual production of around 60 million litres. The Swan Valley was the first area to be planted in 1829, and dominated production until the 1970s with its fortified wines. Since then, new areas have been planted, led by the Margaret River, which produces some of Australia's best wines. Drought is the main enemy of producers.

Great Southern: Also known as the Mount Barker/Franland River Area, this area's acreage under vine is declining. Produces good Rhine Riesling (2) and Chardonnay (2), and in the reds, Cabernet Sauvignon (D), Shiraz (E) and Pinor Noir (B).

Margaret River: About 200 miles south of Perth, with a worldwide reputation built up in little more than 20 years. Quality is the keynote and many of the wines are of world class.

HOUGHTON

1987
SHIRAZ
FRANKLAND RIVER

12.0% VOL
WINE MADE IN AUSTRALIA 750ml

The Cabernet Sauvignon is a star performer with superb rich fruit and ages wonderfully (D); the Chardonnay is rich, buttery and often barrel-fermented for greater complexity (2); the Sémillon is super-fresh, crisply acid with an appley tang and rich fruit and will age (2); the Rhine Riesling is aromatic, full of flowery fruit and classy, with good acidity (2); the Sauvignon Blanc is clean, crisp and grassy: its wood ageing works wonders (2); the Syrah is big, rich, peppery, matures with elegance and ages well (E); the Pinot Noir is soft and plummy, with berry-fruit taste sensations and will age (B); and the Chenin Blanc is crips and fresh, with good peardrop fruit: drink youngish (2).

Mount Barker: Part of the Lower Great Southern area and noted especially for Cabernet Sauvignon (D), and Rhine Riesling (2).

Swan Valley: The vineyards follow the Swan River in one of the world's hottest wine regions. Originally a producer of beefy reds and heavy whites, it is now noted for softer, lighter styles. Fresh, crips fruity Chenin Blanc (2), Chardonnay and Sémillon are produced, together with steadily improving Cabernet Sauvignon (D).

QUEENSLAND and other areas

Wine has been produced in Queensland for almost 150 years and there are still almost a score of vineyards, covering about 375 acres. Most of the vineyards are in the cooler south, close to the New South Wales border in what is known as the Granite Belt. The state's most famous wine is a Beaujolais Nouveau-style, based on Shiraz, or sometimes Cabernet Sauvignon. It is known as Ballandean Nouveau, and is named after the town in the heart of the Granite Belt. Other wines produced include Chardonnay, Sauvignon Blanc, Sémillon, Rhine Riesling and Pinot Noir. Liqueur Muscats are also produced.

Alice Springs in the Northern Territory has a single, 7-acre vineyard, Chateau Hornsby, which must be the hottest and most isolated in the world. It produces Cabernet Sauvignon, Shiraz, Rhine Riesling and Sémillon but a lot of the wine is brought in from other regions and blended.

TASMANIA

The first vineyard was planted in 1823 and the wine industry flourished for about 50 years when it died out. A French engineer working on a hydro-electric scheme planted the first vineyards this century in the late 1950s. Today there are about 15 wineries in the Hobart and Launceston areas, producing wines known for their aromas and fragrance. Best wines are from Chardonnay (2), Pinot Noir (B) and Rhine Riesling (2). Enormous potential for fine, sparkling wine.

Gumpoldskirchner
Winzergenossenschaft

Dr. Lueger

SPATROT-ROTGIPFLER
Qualitätswein mit staatl. Prüfnr. W 0088789

ALC 12% VOL.

℮ 750 ML
TROCKEN

PRODUCED AND BOTTLED IN AUSTRIA

A-2352 GUMPOLDSKIRCHEN, JUBILÄUMSSTR. 43

Imported by: CAXTON TOWER WINES LTD. LONDON, SW6 6BE

Austria

History: One of Europe's oldest wine countries,
with the vineyards first planted by the Romans. In
AD 955 Otto I ordered the church to replant its
vineyards, and the wine, mostly from the large
monastic estates in Bavaria and Salzburg, was known
as Österweine. In the 16th century, Hungary came
under Ottoman rule and wine-making was
outlawed. Austria underwent a massive vineyard
expansion as it tried to take Hungary's place. It is
estimated that there were more than 1,500,000 acres
of vineyards in the mid-16th century, about ten
times the present acreage.

Current situation: Austria is best known for its
crisp, dry whites and luscious, sweet dessert wines
which rival those of Germany but are much more
affordable. It is gradually recovering from the illegal
additives scandal which broke in 1985 and
fortunately, has managed to retain much of its
reputation for fine wines, epecially the dessert wines.

Traditional varieties are being augmented by
plantings of Cabernet Sauvignon and Chardonnay.
There are about 150,000 acres of vineyard producing
about 300 million litres of wine a year – about 90%
white and 10% red – most of which is consumed on
the home market.

Classification: New wine laws similar to Germany's
were introduced in 1985/6. Varietal wines must be at
least 85 per cent of the grape named on the label.
The label must indicate the degree of sweetness:
trocken (dry), halbtrocken (half dry), halbsüss or
liebich (medium sweet), and süss (very sweet).
Export wines carry a banderol and registration on
every bottle.
Tafelwein is the lowest-quality category, and most
not be higher than $11\frac{1}{2}°$, often blended from several
regions.
Landwein is one up from Tafelwein and the grapes
must come from a single region. The wine must be
dry.
Qualitätswein means that grapes must come from
one region and only specified grape varieties are
permitted. Alcohol and sweetness is controlled and
the wines must pass government analytic tests.
Kabinett is as above but dryish. Added sugar is not
allowed.
Prädikatswein is the highest category and sub-
divided into groups according to sweetness, which
depends on when the grapes were picked (the later
the harvesting, the sweeter the grape). The groups
start with Spätlese, the driest, and progress through
Auslese, Eiswein, Beerenauslese and Ausbruch to
Trochenbeerenauslese. The divisions are the same as
in Germany, except for Ausbruch, which is peculiar
to Austria.

Grapes and Styles: the number of native grape
varieties has been reduced from about 200 to 33 in
order to raise quality. There are increasing plantings
of classic varieties such as Cabernet: Sauvignon,
Cabernet Franc, Merlot and Chardonnay but local
varieties still predominate.

Reds: *Blaufränkisch*: soft tartness with a fruity bouquet. Improves with age (B).

Blauer Zweigelt: fruity, lively when young, mellow and velvety when aged (B).

Blauer Portugieser: mild, easy drinking. Drink young.

Whites: *Gründer Veltliner*: the most planted variety, with fruity bouquet and spicy, racy flavour. Can be spritzy. Drink young (3).

Riesling: delicate, clean, fresh, fragrant with a hint of peaches. Ages well (2/9).

Welschriesling: fruity, fresh with a flowery bouquet. Drink youngish (3).

Weissburgunder (Pinot Blanc): full bodied, dry, steely. Improves with age (3).

Neuburger: full-bodied, smooth with a nutty flavour. Drink youngish (3).

Muskat-Ottonel: mild, with a fine bouquet and ripe fruit. Ages well (8).

Müller-Thurgau: soft, with a flowery bouquet, spicy. Low acidity. Drink young (4).

Gewürztraminer: full-bodied, with a heavy bouquet, spicy. Will age (4).

Zierfandler: full-bodied, heavy, fiery, zesty. Ages well (4).

GRÜNER VELTLINER
WEINVIERTEL

1989

ESTATE BOTTLED
NIEDERÖSTERREICHISCHER WINZERVERBAND – VIENNA
AUSTRIA
QUALITÄTSWEIN MIT STAATL. PRÜFNUMMER

ALC 11,5% VOL.   e 750 ML

Q

PLATZEN-NR.
033500

Graf Bubna

NUSSDORFER GRÜNER VELTLINER
KABINETT
11% ALK./VOL.   1984   TROCKEN
Bubna-Litic, Gutsverwaltung in Nußdorf

Regions: the main vineyards are in the east, close to the borders with Czechoslovakia, Hungary and Yugoslavia.

Lower Austria: A warm, mild region producing quality whites and reds. It includes the sub-regions of Kamptal-Donauland, Donauland-Carnuntum, Wachau and Weinviertel.

Vienna: Surrounding the capital and mainly producing young wines sold in Heurigen (wine bars). The wine is often drawn from the cask and must be sold within a year of the harvest.

Burgenland: Includes the important Neusiedlersee vineyards noted for top quality whites, Neusiedlersee-Hugelland and Mittelburgenland, both noted for reds, and Südburgenland, noted for fine reds and the best Welschriesling.

Styria: The most southerly wine region, influenced by the southern European climate. Sub-regions are southern Styria, noted for rich-flavoured whites, Western Styria, noted Schilcher rosé, and south-east Styria, which produces the best Traminer and Gewürztraminer wines.

Brazil

History: The first vineyards were planted by Portuguese settlers, although there was no significant acreage until the turn of this century. A wave of Italian immigrants after the First World War created a major vineyard expansion in the 1920s.

Current situation: A huge wine-producing country with more than 160,000 acres of vineyards. The third largest in South America, with about 12,000 acres planted with classic varieties, particularly Cabernet Sauvignon and Chardonnay. Main varieties are native American 'labrusca' varieties. Leading foreign companies have been largely responsible for modernising the country's wine industry. There are no wine laws and most of the wines are best drunk young. Soft, fruity reds are being produced with some ageing and these hold out promise of longer-living, sturdier reds.

Regions: Rio Grande do Sul is the main region, close to the Uruguay border and famous for the Palomas district which produces some of the best export wines, both varietals and attractive blends. Classic varieties include Cabernet Sauvignon, Cabernet Franc, Pinot Noir, Merlot, Chardonnay, Riesling, Sauvignon Blanc, Chenin Blanc and Muscat. Other wine areas include: Sao Paulo, Santa Catarina, Minas Gerais and Rio de Janeiro.

Styles: *Reds*: *Merlot/Cabernet Franc blend*: soft, rich fruit with a full flavour. Drink young (B).
Cabernet Sauvignon: soft, smooth, rich curranty fruit. Drink young (C).
Merlot: soft, velvety fruit, very smooth. Drink young (B).
Whites: *Chenin Blanc*: good acidity and fruity, slightly honeyed flavour. Drink young (4).
Chardonnay: light style, with buttery, fruity flavour. Drink young (2).

Bulgarian Welschriesling

RUSSE REGION

A fresh medium white wine

Produced and bottled by Vinprom Russe
Exported by Vinimpex, Sofia

11.5% vol   e 75cl

BULGARIA VINO·BИHO

UK importer   BULGARIAN (BVC) VINTNERS Co Ltd   N1 9RD

Bulgaria

History: Bulgaria has been producing wine for the best part of 3,000 years and many believe it is the cradle of wine-making. Although wine-making was outlawed during the centuries of Ottoman rule, many vineyards were maintained and regional Turkish governors planted large acreages for table grapes. The vineyard acreage shot up after the First World War and by 1938 production topped 200 million litres a year, about a third of which was exported to Germany. The industry was devastated during the Second World War and a huge replanting programme was undertaken in 1948.

Current situation: Bulgaria is now the world's fourth largest wine exporter. It is a mountainous country in the eastern Balkans, bordering Greece and Turkey to the south, Yugoslavia to the west, Romania to the north and the Black Sea to the east. There are more than 450,000 acres of vineyards and production tops 400 million litres a year, split evenly between whites and reds, and 85 per cent is

exported. All styles of wine are produced, as well as a wide range of vermouths and spirits.
Bulgaria is the fifth largest wine shipper to the UK and its Cabernet Sauvignon is Britain's best-selling red wine.

Classification: There are three gradings. Lowest in quality are wines of declared variety or brand. Next come wines of declared geographical origin (DGO). These are of higher quality, with production strictly controlled. Controliran wines, from specific varieties grown in specific areas, are the highest in quality. The best of Controliran and DGO wines can be offered as aged Reseve wines and, in exceptional years only, as Special Reserves.

Grapes: Extensive recent plantings of imported classic varieties – Cabernet Sauvignon, Merlot and Chardonnay – form the backbone of exports. Other imported varieties include Riesling, Aligote and Ugni Blanc.
Indigenous varieties include Gamza, Melnik and Mavrud (reds), and Rkatziteli, Dimiat and Misket (whites).

Styles: *Reds*: *Cabernet Sauvignon*: intense colour, rich with curranty fruit. Ages well. Those from northern regions have slightly more elegance (D).
Merlot: soft, rich, plummy, damson fruit, drink youngish. The best age well (B).
Gamza: rich, with vibrant fruit, spicy, complex and mellow with age (D).
Melnik: dryish, with tobacco aromas, soft fruit, complex. Ages well (D).
Mavrud: big, powerful, with rich fruit. Ages well (D).
Whites: *Country wines*: good value blends, with good fruits and flavour. Drink young (2-4/A-C).
Aligote: crisp, with refreshing acidity and ripe fruit. Drink young (1).
Chardonnay: dry, buttery, lemony, soft fruit, with/without oak. Drink youngish. The best come from Khan Krum (2).
Sauvignon Blanc: aromatic, soft, dry and easy drinking. Drink young (1).

Assenovgrad
1985
Mavrud

ASSENOVGRAD
REGION

A full bodied red wine

Exported by Vinimpex, Sofia
Produced and bottled by Vinprom Plovdiv
at Assenovgrad Winery

12% vol

e75cl

UK importer BULGARIAN (BVC) VINTNERS c-td. N1 9D

Recommended wineries from the five wine-producing areas:

Eastern: Burgas, Shumen, Novi Pazar, Preslav, Targovishte, Khan Krum, Kralevo.

Northern: Novo Selo, Pleven, Lositza, Svishtov, Pavlikeni, Suhindol, Russe, Ljaskovetz, Russenski Briag.

Southern: Brestnik, Assenovgrad, Stambolovo, Sakar, Oriachovitza, Plovdiv, Haskovo, Sliven, Chirpan, and Perishitza.

South-West: Melnik, Harsovo, Blagoevgrad.

Sub-Balkan: Sungulare and Rozovo Dolina.

WHITE WINE   VIN BLANC

DOMAINE D'OR

Supérieur Dry

A flavourful, dry white wine with
a pale straw colour.

750 mL 11.5% alc./vol.

BOTTLED UNDER LICENCE FROM GUILLAUME M. DUMONS, CHAGNY (S&L) FRANCE BY

MAISON DOMAINE D'OR

TRURO, ST-HYACINTHE, WINONA, MORRIS, CALGARY, PORT MOODY, CANADA
PRODUCT OF CANADA · PRODUIT DU CANADA

Canada

History: Legend has it that when the Vikings
discovered Canada they called it Vineland because
there were so many vines. Almost certainly the vines
were bearing berries not grapes, and it is thought
that the first wine was made by French missionaries
in the late 16th century. Commercial wine-making
started in the early 1800s with John Schiller, a former
corporal in the German Army. By the turn of the
century there were about 5,000 acres of vines on the
Niagara Peninsula. The first vines in British
Columbia were planted in the 1920s by a Hungarian
but until the 1960s, many of the west coast wineries
made wine with grapes imported from California.
Regulations were then introduced to ensure that
local grapes accounted for most of the wine.

Current situation: The 25,000 acres of vineyards
are now concentrated in Southern Ontario around
the Niagara Falls (22,500 acres), and on the west
coast in British Columbia (2,500 acres). There is a
sprinkling of vineyards in other provinces.

Total production is now about 70 million litres a year from mainly North American varieties but classic and experimental varieties are increasing. Table wines, which account for about 90 per cent of production, have taken over from the previously more popular sweet, dessert wines. Most table wines are blends of different vintages and most are wood-aged.

Classification: Ontario has introduced a Vintners' Quality Alliance (VGA) to control varieties, region, yields, methods of wine-making and so on for its finer wines. Standards have improved and there are a handful of outstanding wineries, but under the new free trade agreement, competition from the US will be intense and producers can only survive by going for quality.

Regions and Styles:

Ontario
This province produces between 85–90 per cent of
Canada's wine grapes. North American Labrusca
varieties, Concord, Niagara and Elvira, have
predominated, with French hybrids such as De
Chaunac becoming more popular. Classic varieties
such as Aligoté, Chardonnay, Gamay,
Gewürztraminer, Riesling and Pinot Noir have all
been planted with varying degrees of success largely
due to the harsh climate.
Most of the vineyards are on the Niagara Peninsula
although there are some south of Toronto.
All styles of wine are produced from apertif, table
and dessert, to sparkling and fortified. The trend is
towards dryer table wines. Local varieties are often
recognised by their 'foxy' taste and classic varieties
show most promise.

Reds: dry, light, freh and fruity, with some good
Pinot Noir and Gamay. Drink youngish (B).
Whites: light, aromatic and flowery, with some good
Chardonnay and Riesling. Drink young, although
best wines age well (2/3).

British Columbia
The Okanagan Valley is home to the BC vineyards,
which specialised in sweet, port-style wines,
although classic/hybrid varieties are increasing with
some good results.

Reds: deep-coloured and light-bodied, with low
acidity; fruity and aromatic. The best will age (B/C).
Whites: at their best good and crisp, with acidity and
fruity aromas. Drink young. Good Riesling,
Gewurztraminer, Chenin Blanc (2).

Vin Blanc   White Wine

Hochtaler

A quality dry table wine
artfully vinted from selected grapes offering a clean,
balanced taste. Serve well chilled.

PRODUCT OF CANADA/PRODUIT DU CANADA

11% alc./vol.

1L

+166005

ANDRÉS WINES LTD., TRURO, ST-HYACINTHE, WINONA, MORRIS, CALGARY, PORT MOODY, CANADA

Chile

History: Vines were introduced by the first Spanish
missionaries in the 1530s and the first sizeable
plantings were around Santiago in the mid 1550s,
mostly of Muscat for communion wines. Silvestre
Ochagavia is regarded as the father of Chilean wine.
He imported French varieties and French vineyard
and winery experts. Vineyards established in Central
Chile were so successful the government took over
the project, expanding the acreage and building the
wineries.

Current situation: Chile is south America's best
wine producer, one of the most exciting of all the
'new' wine countries, and some of its exports are
stunning. There are about 275,000 acres of
vineyards, producing about 600 million litres of
wine a year, of which less than 5 per cent is exported.
Chile has a number of things going for it. Its vines
are mostly free of disease and naturally protected
from threat by the Pacific and the Andes. The
climate and soil are ideal for vines and almost all the

production is of an acceptable standard, with some of it outstanding. The trend now is to replant vineyards in the most favourable sites, especially in the cooler areas south of Santiago, Miguel Torres, son of the Penedés Torres, has done most to revitalise the country's wine industry and his results have been the catalyst to bring in much more foreign investment and master wine-makers. Investment in wineries and cellars has led to marvellous cool fermentation whites and fruity, full-flavoured reds aged in small oak barrels. Generally, fortified wines are made in the north, the finest table wines in the central region, and good, evryday table wines in the south.

Classification: There is a general Denominación de Origen which divides the country into four areas: Mailp, Rapel, Maule and Bio-Bio, which are themselves sub-divided into 31 denominacíones. These titles simply indicate the area of origin and are not concerned with quality. According to regulations one-year-old wines should be labelled 'courant', two-year-olds as 'special', four-year-olds as 'reserve' and six-year-olds and older as 'gran Vino'. These

CABERNET - SAUVIGNON
ANTIGUAS RESERVAS
GRAN VINO
EMBOTELLADO EN ORIGEN POR VIÑA COUSIÑO MACUL · SANTIAGO-CHILE
Producto Chileno
Contenido 750 ml   Produce of Chile   Alcohol 12°

terms are much abused and in reality mean little. Total yields are controlled, although harvests are massive by European standards. White wines must not exceed 12° and reds 11½°.

Grapes: The varieties offering most promise are classical varieties. Cabernet Sauvignon is the main red variety, followed by Merlot and a little Malbec, with Chardonnay the main white, followed by Sauvignon Blac and Sémillon. There are increasing acreages of Riesling, Gewürztraminer and other European whites.

Regions: *Central Valley*, is the most important region for quality wines with Cabernet Sauvignon (D), Chardonnay (2) and Sémillon (2) all showing very well. This area includes the valleys of the Maipo, Cachapoal, Lontué and Maule, all with good vineyards.

DOMAINE

CAPERANA

Isla de Maipo

Sauvignon Blanc

CANEPA

CHILE

12% vol
750 ml

Produce of Chile
Bottled by Jose Canepa & Co. Ltd., Maipú, Chile
exclusively for Direct Wines (Windsor) Ltd,
Reading RG4 0JY. UK ,the importer

Other regions: Aconcagua Valley (good Cabernet Sauvignon, Chardonnay and Sauvignon Blanc), Colchagua Valley, Curico, Nancagua and Peumo. Santa Ana was the first Chilean grower to export to the USA in 1912. Chilean exports to the UK have risen from 20,000 cases to more than 250,000 in the last three years.

Styles: *Reds*: *Cabernet Sauvignon*: full-bodied, rich blackcurranty fruit, good tannin and soft oak. Drink Youngish, but it will age (d).
Malbec: full, rich and fruity. Drink youngish (D).
Merlot: Soft and velvety with good fruit. Drink youngish (B).
Whites: *Chardonnay*: fresh, crisp, buttery and lingering. Drink youngish but will age (2).
Sauvignon Blanc: fresh, ripe and fruity with a hint of grapefruit. Drink young (1).

DRAGON SEAL®
MEDIUM DRY WINE

12%Vol   Produced and bottled in CHINA by a Sino-French joint venture
          BEIJING FRIENDSHIP WINERY CO. LTD.   75cl

China

History: China has to be mentioned because its
wine making tradition is at least 2,000 years old and
it does export its wines; although its vineyard acreage
is now much reduced as the locals prefer rice wine.
There are thought to be about 50,000 acres of vines,
with a variety of Asian, American and European
varieties introduced over the years. Attempts were
made to revitalise the industry in the 1970s and early
1980s with French investment and expertise, which
produced the Dynasty range of wines. There have
been plantings most of the classic European varieties
and new winery techniques can greatly improve local
varieties such as Beichun and Dragon Eye. Best
export results to date have been with Chardonnay
and Riesling although there have been one or two
passable attempts with lightish Cabernet Sauvignon.
There is still some way to go!

Regions: Hebei, Henan, Jiangsu, Liaoning, Shanxi,
Shantung and Sinkiang.

Cyprus

History: The wine-making tradition here dates back
4,000 years. Vineyards were planted by the Greeks,
the Phoenicians and the Romans. Wines produced
were exported to ancient Egypt, Athens and Rome.
Wines produced were exported to ancient Egypt,
Athens and Rome. Britain has been importing
Cypriot wines for almost 1,000 years and Queen
Elizabeth I granted Sir Walter Raleigh the exclusive
right to import them into Britain. The vines have
also been exported and are thought to be the source
of Madeira, and of Hungarian Tokay and Marsala.
Wine-making diminished greatly but did not die
out under the Ottoman rule. It was not really revived
until 1878, when the island was ceded to Britain.

Current situation: Today there are more than
65,000 acres under vines. The most famous wine is
Commanderia St.John, one of the world's oldest
(first recorded in 1191), a massive, sweet dessert wine
made from sun-dried grapes and matured in barrels
exposed to the sun's heat. With the loss of the

traditional Cyprus Sherry market, vineyards have been replanted, wineries modernised and growers are concentrating on producing light, aromatic, fruity table wines. The industry is dominated by the four main wineries – Etko, Keo, Loel and Sodap. All are based in Limassol, although Keo has built small wineries closer to its best vineyards. The government's experimental winery is leading the way in developing more suitable grape varieties and more commercial styles for export.

Classification: Wine-growing areas have been designated and graded according to quality. Commanderia, produced in 14 mountain villages, has already been accorded Appellation Controllée status. Other regions and individual wines will follows.

MEDIUM DRY FRUITY WHITE

Cyprus Wine

70 cl ℮

IMPORTED BY WOOLLEY, DUVAL AND BEAUFOYS LTD., KINGSTON UPON THAMES.
PRODUCED AND BOTTLED BY KEO LTD, LIMASSOL, CYPRUS.

Grapes: the main grape varieties are: *Mavro* (about 70 per cent of all plantings), *Xynisteri*, *Opthalmo* and *Muscat*. The main classic varieties are: *Cabernet Sauvignon*, *Cabernet Franc*, *Carignan*, *Grenache*, *Palomino*, *Chardonnay* and *Riesling*.

Regions: around Paphos and Limassol, mainly on the southern slopes of the Troodos Mountains, with a small area around Nicosia.

Styles: *Reds*: light, dry, fruity and mellow, to be drunk young (C), or full-bodied, with rich fruit and firmness when aged. Drink youngish (E).
Commanderia: rich, sweet and long lasting (9).
Whites: Cool-fermented to produce generally light, dry, crisp wines, retaining natural aromas and flavours. There are more full-bodied wines available and refreshing, naturally spritzy whites. Drink young (2/3).
Sweet whites: light and rounded, with good fruit and acidity to balance sweetness (7).

Czechoslovakia

History: There are records of wine-making in Bohemia in the 9th century and vines were imported from Burgundy in the 14th century following an edict by Emperor Charles IV. In the 16th century Bohemia was a major wine-producing area, especially around Prague, but the Thirty Years War devastated the vineyards and wineries, and troubles over the next two centuries blocked repeated attempts to replant. Modern wine-making dates back to the 1920s, when a massive programme of replanting was undertaken.

Current situation: Annual production is about 140 million litres a year from about 135,000 acres of vineyards. Most of the wine is blended and drunk at home but the first major exports – of classic varietal wines – will be launched in the UK in 1991.

Grapes: *Whites*: Rhine Riesling, Pinot Blanc, Gruner Veltliner, Müller-Thurgau, Traminer, Gewürztraminer, Sylvaner, Sauvignon Blanc and Muscat Ottonel. *Main reds*: Limberger, Cabernet Sauvignon, Blauburgunder and Portugieser.

Regions: The main wine-producing areas are Moravia, in the middle of the country and Slovakia in the east bordering Hungary, which includes part of the Tokay region. Boehmia in the west produces small quantities of German-style whites. Producers are concentrating on quality varietals for the export market. Pinot Noir, Sauvignon Blanc and Traminer show the most promise.

1987
BACCHUS

NUTBOURNE MANOR

Grown by and bottled for Nutbourne Manor Vineyard.
Nutbourne Manor, Nutbourne, Nr Pulborough, Sussex.

ENGLISH TABLE WINE

70 cl ℮   Produce of the United Kingdom.   11.5 %vol

The smiling Bacchus to Ariadne, after a marble figure by Joseph Coit.

England

History: Wine-making dates back to the latter end
of the first century AD and the first vines were
planted by Roman officials on their villa estates.
When the Romans began to leave at the beginning
of the 5th century, the vineyards went into decline
and many disappeared. There was a revival of wine-
making in the 9th century and by the time of the
Norman Conquest, wine was produced in most
counties in southern England. The Vikings imported
many vines from the Rhine and the Normans
introduced French varieties. From 1066, wine-
making was in the hands of the monasteries until the
Dissolution in the 1530s. Thereafter, many of the
vineyards were given to nobles, who brought in
European experts to improve the quality of wine-
making. Wine-making continued at a reduced scale
until the First World War, when the vineyards were
cleared to grow crops. The modern revival didn't get
under way until the 1950s but the acreage has
increased steadily since then, as has the quality of
wine produced.

Current situation: There are now about 300
commercial vineyards, covering 2,200 acres and
expanding fast. The vineyards are among the most
northerly in the world and weather is the constant
enemy. The 1989 vintage was rated the best of the
century and yielded 4 million bottles. The 1990
vintage was massive and again proved that English
wines of high quality can be made in viable
quantities. Most wine sold is blended white, and can
range from dry to sweet, although there is a trend
towards dryer varietals. The quality of reds,
particularly Pinot Noir is steadily improving, and
there are some good sparkling wines made,
including Methode Champenoise.

Classification: The English wine industry is too
young to have an EC-recognised quality system, but
the English Vineyards Association, which was
formed in 1965, runs a 'Seal of Quality' scheme. It
started in 1978, and wines have to pass strict analysis
and tasting before being accorded the Seal. Each year
about 60–70 wines qualify.

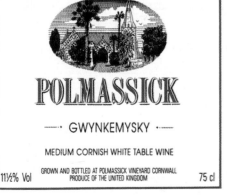

POLMASSICK

--- · GWYNKEMYSKY · ---

MEDIUM CORNISH WHITE TABLE WINE

11½% Vol   GROWN AND BOTTLED AT POLMASSICK VINEYARD CORNWALL
PRODUCE OF THE UNITED KINGDOM   75 cl

SHAWSGATE

FRAMLINGHAM CASTLE

English Table Wine

ESTATE BOTTLED BY
SHAWSGATE VINEYARD · FRAMLINGHAM · SUFFOLK

10.5% vol   PRODUCE OF U.K.   75 cle

Grapes: Because England enjoyed 'experimental status' under EEC wine laws for many years, a wide range of varieties – mostly white – were planted. Main varieties today are: Müller Thurgau (the most planted variety), Seyval Blanc, Reichensteiner, Schönburger, Bacchus, Huxelrebe, Madelaine Angevine, Kerner and Ortega. Pinot Noir is the most planted red variety.

Regions: Most of the vineyards are located in the South of England and East Anglia although they extend into the Midlands and the furthest north is just outside Leeds in Yorkshire. There are also a handful of vineyards in Wales, the Channel Islands and Ireland.

Styles: *Bacchus*: crisp, floral and fruity with a hint of elderflowers. Drink young (2/4).
Huxelrebe: fat, grapefruity, often blended for softening effect. Drink young (2/4).
Madelaine Angevine: crisp and fruity with good acidity; can be honeyed. Drink youngish (2/4).

Müller Thurgau: aromatic and flowery with hints of gooseberry. Drink youngish (2/4).

Ortega: big, fruity and off-dry with a hint of elderflower. Drink youngish (2/4).

Pinot Noir: for rosé and light reds, delicate and fruity. Will age.

Reichensteiner: floral, with elderflower and a rich fruity palate. Will age (2/4).

Scheurebe: strong, grapefruity flavours; floral and aromatic. Drink young (2/4).

Schönburger: soft and perfumed, with peachy, pear flavours. Drink youngish (2/4).

Seyval Blanc: crisp, with grapefruit flavours when young. Ages well (2/4).

Note: English wine is wine made in England from grapes grown here and should not be confused with British wine, which is made from imported grapes, often from Algeria and elsewhere.

GRANDE CUVÉE
1982

CHATEAU DE BEAULIEU

MIS EN BOUTEILLE AU CHATEAU

COTEAUX D'AIX-EN-PROVENCE
APPELLATION D'ORIGINE
VIN DÉLIMITÉ DE QUALITÉ SUPÉRIEURE

TOUZET - GFA DU CHATEAU DE BEAULIEU
Propriétaire-récoltant à Rognes (B.-du-Rh.)

37,5 cl

FRANCE

France

History: The first cultivated vines were probably planted by the Greeks around Marseille, although it was the Romans who, over the course of 500 years, introduced the wine making tradition throughout the country. Experimentation with vines and wine making techniques took place hundreds of years ago, and people now generally accept which areas produce the best grapes, what varieties are most suited to them, how they should be trained and so on.

Current situation: Today, France can boast more great wines than any other nation, and the grape varieties used to produce them have been exported around the globe setting the standards for others. Apart from the prestige areas of Bordeaux, Burgundy, Champagne, Rhône and the Loire, there are scores of other areas where the quality of wine has improved almost beyond recognition in the past two decades, and which have not been hit by the rocketing prices which have put many top-name wines out of the reach of most consumers.

Buyers for wine merchants and supermarkets are increasingly turning to these lesser-known regions for their supplies, and the growers are only too keen to provide quality wine at affordable prices. Overall, the average harvest is about 7,600 million litres.

Classification: *AC (or AOC): Appellation Contrôlée (or Appellation d'Origine Contrôlée):* The highest quality category. There are about 400 ACs producing about 2,100 million litres of wine a year – about 28–29 per cent of France's total production. Just under a third is exported. Each AC covers a specific area, where the wine is produced, and regulations dictate grape varieties grown, how they are cultivated, yields to be harvested, wine making techniques and alcoholic strength. While the AC will always guarantee the origin of the wine it does not necessarily guarantee its quality.
VDQS: Vin Délimité de Qualité Supérieure: 'Apprentice' AC wines, which have to comply with the same regulations although yields can be higher and alcoholic strength lower. Most VDQS wines are striving for AC status and many have already achieved it, which is why production is just a little over 1 per cent of total wine production in France. About a fifth of all VDQS wine is exported.

TOUZET G.F.A. CHATEAU DE BEAULIEU · 13840 ROGNES · FRANCE

Vin de Pays: These wines account for between 12 and 14 per cent of total production and about 10 per cent is exported. The classification was introduced to persuade growers to raise standards, and the wines are often referred to as 'French Country Wines'. There are three sub-categories specifying where the wine comes from – a local area (*Vins de Pays de Zone*) – often the best; a Département (Vins de Pays Départementaux); or more than one Département (Vin de Pays Régionaux).

Vin de Table wines account for almost half of France's total production. Also known as *vins ordinaires*, they are everyday drinking wines. About 12 per cent is exported and although quality varies enormously there are great bargains to be found.

MIS EN BOUTEILLE AU CHATEAU

Château de Beaulieu

Regions and Grapes
ALSACE

Alsace lies in the eastern corner of France,
sandwiched between the Rhine in the east and the
foothills of the Vosges in the west, with Switzerland
to the south and Germany to the north east. This
region runs for 90 miles along the border and has
been fought over for centuries. Historical links
explain why the wine making techniques are similar
to those of the Rhine and why local names often
appear Germanic. There are about 30,000 acres of
vineyards, which in good years produce about 150
million bottles.

Alsace is unique in France because usually all wines
are labelled according to the seven main grape
varieties used. Where this is specified the wine is
made 100 per cent from that variety.

Grapes: *Gewürztraminer*: Rich, spicy, aromatic, mouth-filling exotic fruitiness often camouflages its underlying dryness. Mellows beautifully with age (4).

Muscat: Dry, very light and full of fresh grapey flavour. Best drunk young, and a great aperitif (1).

Pinot Blanc: Light, fruity and crisp with hint of apple. Has good acidity so keeps well for a few years, especially when wood-aged (3).

Pinot Gris (Tokay d'Alsace): A great big, rich wine, sumptious and honeyed from fruit which masks the underlying dryness. Good vintages will keep for years (2).

Pinot Noir: Light, fresh and fruity. Best drunk young, but has ageing potential (B).

Riesling: Dry, steely and crisp when young; developing into a luscious, oily wine of great complexity with ageing (2).

Sylvaner: Fresh, fruity and crisp, with high acidity, giving a refreshing quality. It can often have a slight fizz. It doesn't age well, although time in oak gives it more body and depth (2).

Some special Alsace classifications: *Crémand d'Alsace*: A dry, sparkling wine made from Pinot Blanc, sometimes with a little Riesling. Flowery, fruity and refreshing (2).
Grand Cru: A title conferred on the best growers.
Réserve: A term used by growers to denote their best wines.
Sélection de Grains Nobles: Only used in exceptional vintages to denote grapes with very high sugar content which produce luscious, sweet wines (8).
Spécial: Another term used by growers to distinguish their best wines.
Vendange Tardive: Late-picked grapes with high sugar quality, which produce either dry, alcohol-high wines, or rich, sweet wines, though not quite so luscious as *Sélection de Grains Nobles*.

Best recent vintages: 1989, 1988, 1985, 1983, 1981.

BORDEAUX

The Gironde, in south west France, is the country's largest Département, and the home of Bordeaux wines, including claret, Britain's favourite French wine for centuries. But while all claret is Bordeaux, not all Bordeaux is claret.

Bordeaux is the largest area of fine wine production – red, white and dessert – in the world. The vines cover more than 500 square miles, split almost evenly between red and white grapes, and most of the wines have AC status. The vineyards run from the west bank of the Gironde estuary southwards to below the River Garonne.

There are more than 250,000 acres of vineyards producing an average of 600 million bottles a year. There are 53 ACs, more than 10,000 Châteaux, more than 2,000 properties and more than 40 *caves cooperatives*. The very best wines are classified into 'Growths' or '*Crus*', and are needless to say, very expensive. *Crus Bourgeois* is the next quality category and offers many of the best bargains.

Bordeaux Red

Grapes: *Cabernet Sauvignon*: Tannic, blackcurranty wines which soften with ageing. *Cabernet Franc*: Good blackcurrant fruit but lighter and softer than Sauvignon. Usually blended. *Merlot*: Produces plummy, blackcurranty, softer, easier drinking wines. *Malbec*: Produces soft, low acidic wines almost always blended.

Classifications and styles: *Bordeaux*: Young and fruity, everyday drinking wines from anywhere in the region (C). *Bordeaux Supérieur*: As above, but with slightly higher alcohol level (C). *Côte de Blaye*: Light and fruity, everyday drinking wines. Drink young (C). *Côtes de Bourg*: Good, everyday drinking reds, good fruit and high tannin (C). *Côtes de Castillon*: Full-bodied, fruity, with traces of Merlot mintiness. Age well (D). *Côtes de Fronsac*: Good value, full, firm, spicy flavour. Age well (C).

Graves: Improving all the time. Soft, silky, firm, rich and fruity. Age well (C).

Haut-Médoc: Good value, very dry, firm, fruity wines, medium/full-bodied with good ageing potential (C).

Lalande-de-Pomerol: Big, rich wines, full of flavour and character, often nearing Pomerol in quality but at a fraction of the price. Age well (C).

Listrac: Medium-to full-bodied, soft but full of fruit. Age well (C).

Margaux: Need plenty of time (at least 10 years) to develop into perfumed fragrant, delicate wines. Age well for decades in best vintages (C).

Médoc: Made to drink young with Merlot blended in for fruit and softness (C).

Pauillac: Big, intense, blackcurranty fruit with wonderful balance. Expensive. Harsh when young but ages well and is the longest lasting of the clarets (C).

Pessac-Léognan: A new AC covering the best of the Graves (C).

CHÂTEAU DE TRINQUEVEDEL

1989

TAVEL

APPELLATION TAVEL CONTRÔLÉE

MIS EN BOUTEILLE AU CHÂTEAU

Alc. 13% vol.   e 750 ml

S.C.E.A. DE TRINQUEVEDEL - 30126 TAVEL - FRANCE

PRODUCE OF FRANCE

Pomerol: Merlot predominates to give great depth of plummy fruit and softness. Very long lasting. Expensive (C).

Premières Côtes de Blaye: Steadily improving, balanced, plummy jam fruit (C).

Premières Côtes de Bordeaux: Light, fruity-style clarets for easy drinking (C).

St. Emilion: Merlot softness, well balanced, full of fruit and warmth. Ages well (C).

St. Estphe: Strong, robust, full of fruit and flavour. Needs time to develop (C).

St. Julien: Expensive wines of great finesse, full bodied with intense colour and richness of fruit. Age well (C).

Best recent vintages: 1989, 1988, 1986, 1985, 1983, 1982, (1981–78 and 75 have opened up but will continue to improve in good cellars).

Bordeaux White

Grapes: *Sauvignon Blanc*: At its best makes aromatic, herby, crisp, fresh and fruity wines. In blending its acidity adds freshness.

Sémillon: The main variety for Sauternes with a hint of apple on the nose. Produces big, full-bodied, rounded wines which mellow with age and oak into soft, complex wines with hints of citrus fruits and melons, honey and smokiness.

Muscadelle: Used in blending because of its heady perfume and softness.

Regions and styles: *Barsac*: Rich, intense wines with initial sweetness replaced by hint of dryness at the end. Age well (8).

Bordeaux blanc: Dry white wines from anywhere in the Gironde. Drink young (1).

Bordeaux Blanc Supérieur: As above but with higher alcoholic content (1).

Cadillac: sweet, fresh and fruity, floral aromas and honeyed taste. Age well (7).

Cérons: Sweet wine made from late picked, overripe grapes. Age well (7).

Entre-Deux-Mers: Dry whites, crisp, fresh and fruity, grassy (1).

Graves: Much improved of late. The best are dry,
fruity and lively. Drink young (2).

Loupiac: Lush, sweet, full-bodied, often honeyed,
complex and long lasting (7).

Pessac-Léognan: Dry, classy wines from the best
growers in Graves (2).

Premières Côtes de Bordeaux: Good value dry and
sweet wines (1 or 7).

Sainte-Croix-du-Mont: Honeyed, sweet, full-bodied
wines. Long lasting (7).

Sauternes: Strong ($14°\frac{1}{2}$), expensive, luscious,
golden sweet wines. Must be aged and develop
enormous complexity (8).

Best recent vintages: *Dry – 1989, 1988, 1987,
(1986–81 have opened up or reached a certain
maturity but will continue to develop or improve)
Sweet –* 1989, 1988, 1986, 1983, 1980.

BURGUNDY

Burgundy stretches from Chablis, about 114 miles
south east of Paris, southwards along autoroute A6
almost to Lyon. The 75,000 acres of vine include a
number of clearly defined areas – Chablis and the

Auxerrois, Côte de Nuits, Côte de Beaune, Côte Chalonnaise, Macon and Beaujolais. The region is home to many of the world's finest wines, both red and white – and many of the most expensive. Prices of the best wines have rocketed in the last few years, but there are still many bargains to be had.

Classifications: *General appellations*: From anywhere in the region i.e. Bourgogne (Burgundy) Aligote, Bourgogne Rouge.
Regional appellations: Côte de Nuits-Villages or Côte de Beaune Villages
Village or Commune: Appellation Aloxe-Corton
Premier Cru: The best ones name both the vineyard and the village or commune. If the label simply says Premier Cru it is likely to be a blend from a number of top vineyards.
Grand Cru: The top 31 producers, each with their own AC.

Red wines: Grapes: *Pinot Noir*: Burgundy produces some of the world's greatest and finest Pinot Noir wines – light, fragrant, perfumed and with concentrated raspberry/strawberry flavours. Oak ageing adds depth and complexity.
Gamay: The grape for Beaujolais but a little is blended in with Pinot Noir for some Bourgogne wines. It produces light, soft, low tannin, fruity wines generally best drunk young.

ALSACE
APPELLATION
ALSACE
CONTRÔLÉE

ALSACE
PRODUCT
OF
FRANCE

1986

DOPFF & IRION®

GEWURZTRAMINER

Seigneur d'Alsace

MIS EN BOUTEILLE PAR DOPFF & IRION A RIQUEWIHR (H) RHIN.) FRANCE

Shipped by **REYNIER** *London S.W.1*

700 ml

12,5% alc./vol.

Regions and Styles: *Aloxe-Corton (Côte de Beaune)*: Powerful, big and aromatic, with a hint of violets. Harsh when young but mellow wonderfully with age (B).

Auxey-Duresses (Côtes de Beaune): Underrated and good value, full bodied and fruity. Age well (B).

Beaune (Côte de Beaune): Light, soft and fruity with a hint of sweetness. Mature quickly (B).

Blagny (Côtes de Beaune): Big, firm, strong bouquet. Need time to develop (B).

Bonnes-Mares (Côtes de Nuits): Soft and elegant. Need time to mature fully. When aged they give hints of chocolate and prunes (B).

Bourgogne Grand Ordinaire: Quality can vary. At best it is light, perfumed and fruity, often a Pinot Noir-Gamay blend. Best drunk young (C).

Bourgogne Passe-Tout-Grains: Mostly Gamay but at least one third Pinot Noir to give light, fruity wines best drunk young. Generally don't travel well (B).

Bourgogne Rouge: Basic blended red from anywhere in Burgundy. Drink young (B).

Chambertin (Côte de Nuits): Big, lingering wines with deep colour and intense bouquet which soften and mellow with age to become complex, perfumed and rich. The best need at least 10 years to develop (B).

Chambertin Close de Bèze (Côte de Nuits): As above, expensive. Need time (B).

Chambolle-Musigny (Côte de Nuits): Perfumed, light, delicate and elegant. Age well (B).

Charmes-Chambertin (Côte de Nuits): Light and delicate but with body. Age well (B).

Chassagne-Montrachet (Côtes de Beaune): Great value, fine and fruity with earthy flavours. Age well (B).

Chorey-Lés-Beaune (Côte de Beaune): Good value, soft fruit reds. Age well (B).

Close de la Roche (Côtes de Nuits): Big, powerful, complex and full of curranty fruit. Age well (B).

Clos des Lambrays (Côte de Nuits): A new AC: fragrant, fruity and expensive (B).

Clos de Tart (Côte de Nuits): Light, fragrant and fruity. Age well (B).

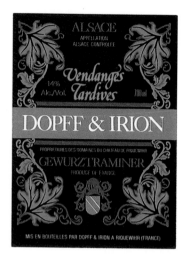

Close de Vougeot (Côte de Nuits): Full-bodied, perfumed, plummy fruit. Age well (B).

Clos St. Denis (Côte de Nuits): Fine, delicate wines of varying quality. Age well (B).

Le Corton (Côte de Beaune): Big, powerful wines which age with great finesse (B).

Côte Chalonnaise: Light and fragrant with intense fruit and finesse. Drink young (B).

Côte de Beaune: Light and soft with good fruit. Mellows with age (B).

Côte de Nuits: Big, firm, fruity wines. Age well (B).

Côte de Nuits Villages: Lighter than above, with earthy flavours. Age well (B).

Echézeaux (Côtes de Nuits): Expensive, light and fragrant. Age well (B).

Fixin (Côte de Nuits): Good value big, strong reds with plummy fruit, which mellow and develop great finesse with age (B).

Gevrey-Chambertin (Côte de Nuits): Big, rich and elegant with silky, plummy fruit when young. Mellows into velvety, perfumed wine with intense fruit. Expensive (B).

Givry (Côte Chalonnaise): Light, soft and fruity, with a strong hint of cherries. Age well (B).

Grands Echézeaux (Côte de Nuits): Expensive complex wines with violet bouquet and soft rich fruit flavour. Develop more intense fruit and bouquet with age (B).

Griotte-Chambertin (Côte de Nuits) Deep-coloured, with soft, intense, cherry fruit. Perfumed and velvety. Age well (B).

Hautes-Côtes de Beaune: Usually good value, light and fruity. Age well (B).

Haute-Côtes de Nuits: Medium to full-bodied, fruity, perfumed wines which age well (B).

Latricières-Chambertin (Côtes de Nuits): Generally big, austere wines which need several years to mature, though some are made lighter for earlier drinking (B).

Macon Rouge: Improved recently. Light, fruity and earthy. Best drunk young (B).

Marsannay (Côtes de Nuits): Big and fruity with a hint of redcurrants. Age well (B).

Mazis-Chambertin (Côtes de Nuits): Silky, delicate and complex. Need time (B).

Mercurey (Côte Chalonnaise): Big with berry fruit flavours, smokey. Good value (B).

Monthélie (Côte de Beaune): Big, firm, fruity wines with long silky finish. Age well (B).

Morey-St.Denis (Côtes de Nuits): Deep colour, big bouquet and full fruity flavour. Age well (B).

Musigny (Côtes de Nuits): Smooth and stylish with velvety fruit. Will keep for ages (B).

Nuits St.George (Côte de Nuits): Has improved recently. Spicy nose and big, rich plummy fruit flavour with touches of sweetness. Age well (B).

Pernand-Vergelesses (Côte de Beaune): Can be silky-smooth and fruity, but often not. Best drunk youngish (B).

Pommard (Côte de Beaune): Big and solid but classy, with plummy fruit. Age well (B).

Richebourg (Côte de Nuits): Big, rich and velvety, with perfumed bouquet, intense fruit flavours and hints of chocolate. Keeps for ages (B).

La Romane (Côte de Nuits): Expensive and classy Pinot which keeps for ages but is not quite so good as the wine below (B).

La Romanée-Conti (Côtes de Nuits): Hugely expensive an fabulously complex (B).

La Romanée-St.Vivant (Côtes de Nuits): Light, elegant and delicious but needs a decade or more to show at its best (B).

Ruchottes-Chambertin (Côtes de Nuits): Expensive, big, rich, fruity long lasting wines (B).

Rully (Côte Chalonnaise): Light, fresh and fruity wines, which mellow with age (B).

St.Aubin (Côte de Beaune): Good value, light and fragrant. Drink youngish (B).

St.Romain (Côte de Beaune): Good value, upfront, fruity reds. Drink young (B).

Santenay (Côte de Beaune): Good value, light, very fruity wines which are quick maturing but last well (B).

Savigny-Ls-Beaune (Côtes de Beaune): Medium bodied, fruity, easy-drinking, good value wines which age well (B).

La Tache (Côtes de Nuits): Very expensive, fabulously rich and complex, silky, perfumed wines that age deliciously (B).

Volnay (Côtes de Beaune): Medium bodied, very perfumed, silky and fruity. Age well (B).

Vosne-Romanée (Côtes de Nuits): Very expensive
and amazingly complex bouquet and flavours. Silky
and classy. Age well (B).
Vougeot (Côtes de Nuits): Expensive, fine but well
balanced. Age well (B).

Best recent vintages: 1989, 1988, 1986 (for most
reds), 1985, 1981.

White Wines: Grapes: *Chardonnay*: The grape
for all the great Burgundy whites. Produces wines of
great balance and finesse with buttery, appley
flavours when young. Côte de Beaune Chardonnay
at its best is dry but the intensity of the fruit gives it
an almost honeyed quality. Oak ageing adds
longevity, character and depth, while new wood
imparts spicy, vanilla characters.
Aligoté: A variety enjoying new popularity.
Produces crisp, refreshing wines best drunk young.
Produces very pleasant slightly sparkling wines.
Melon de Bourgogne: Used in small quantities for
blending in generic wines
Pinot Blanc: Produces well balanced wines with good
acidity. Used in blending
Pinot Buerrot: Used in blending to soften
Chardonnay.

Produce of France

Vin de Pays du Jardin de la France

Chenin

Blanc de Blancs Cépage Chenin

White Table Wine

70 cl

Mis en bouteille à St-Romain-s/-Cher par :
Robert Noël - St-Georges-s/-Cher (Loir-et-Cher) France

REPRODUCTION INTERDITE

S.2

L. RUEL POITIERS

Regions and styles: *Aloxe-Corton (Côtes de Beaune)*: Expensive, big, fat, buttery, and full of flavour. Age well with oak (2).
Auxey-Duresses: (Côtes de Beaune): Soft and nutty flavour. Drink youngish (2).
Batard-Montrachet (Côte de Beaunez): Full-bodied, rich, nutty and honeyed. Age well (2).
Bienvenues-Batard-Montrachet (Côtes de Beaune): Expensive and classy, nutty and honeyed. Develop great complexity with age. Long lasting (2).
Bourgogne Aligoté: Light, dry, crisp and acidic. Drink young (2).
Bourgogne Aligoté de Bouzeron (Côte Chalonnaise): Very dry with a touch of lemon and buttermilk. To be drunk young but ages well in oak (2).
Bourgogne Blanc: Basic white from anywhere in Burgundy but there are bargains, especially wines that have seen some oak (2).
Chassagne-Montrachet (Côte de Beaune): Dry, classy, nutty and full of flavour. Drink youngish (2).
Chevalier-Montrachet (Côte de Beaune): Dry, fat and rich with enormous depth of flavour. Age well (2).

Corton (Côtes de Beaune): Fine, medium-bodied wine full of flavour. Long-lasting (2).

Corton-Charlemagne (Côte de Beaune): Expensive and fabulous. Rich, fat buttery fruit and complex flavour overtones from the oak. Age well (2).

Côte Chalonnaise: Usually light, dry, fresh Chardonnay, occasionally with a little oak age. Drink young (2).

Crémant de Bourgogne: Improving dry, sparkling wine, mostly from Chardonnay. Drink youngish (2).

Criots-Batard-Montrachet (Côtes de Beaune): Expensive and rare, rich, fragrant and honeyed. Last well (2).

Hautes-Côtes de Beaune: Good value, light, dry Chardonnay. Drink young (2).

Hautes-Côtes de Nuits: as above (2).

Macon Blanc: Dry, fresh and fruity Chardonnay. Drink young (2).

Macon-Blanc Villages: Good value, young fresh, easy drinking Chardonnay (2).

Mercurey (Côte Chalonnaise): Dry, light, fresh and stylish. Drink young (2).

Meursault (Côte de Beaune): Big, luscious, nutty and buttery. Last well (2).

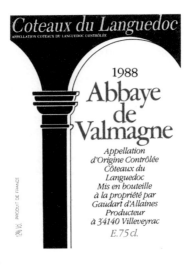

CHAMPAGNE
BOLLINGER
SPECIAL CUVÉE
BRUT

12% Vol.   PRODUCE OF FRANCE   75cl

ELABORÉ PAR BOLLINGER — AY FRANCE

Montagny (Côte Chalonnaise): Lightish and dry.
Better for oak. Drink youngish (2).
Le Montrachet (Côte de Beaune): Fabulous depth
and complexity of flavours. Honeyed, nutty, toasted
and flowery. Ages magnificently for decades (2).
Musigny (Côte de Nuits): Expensive and rare. Rich
fruit but bone dry (2).
Pernand-Vergelesses (Côte de Beaune): Smooth,
light Chardonnays, and excellent, fresh, crisp
Aligot, both to be drunk young (2).
Pouilly-Fuissé (Mâconnais): Balanced, rich and full
bodied. Drink youngish (2).
Puligny-Montrachet (Côte de Beaune): Big, full
bodied and steely dry. Needs time to develop its
nutty, toasted, honey flavours (2).
Rully (Côte Chalonnaise): Crisp, dry and light. Oak
adds fatness. Drink youngish (2).
St.Aubin (Côte de Beaune): Good value, underrated
wines. Dry and full of flavour. Drink youngish (2).
St.Romain (Côte de Beaune): Light, fresh, fruity
Chardonnay. Drink young (2).
St.Véran (Mâconnais): Good value, fresh and fruity
and slightly honeyed. Drink young (2).

Best recent vintages: 1989, 1988, 1986, 1985.

CHABLIS

Grapes: *Chardonnay*: The only grape allowed for
Chablis producing a steely dry, green, acidic wine.
The best wines are much richer, with depth and
intense flavour although still bone dry.
Sauvignon Blanc: Used for Sauvignon de St.Bris.
The variety is not legal in Chablis which is why the
wine has only VDQS status.
Pinot Noir: Mainly used for red wine production,
with some Csar, Gamay and Tressot.

Classifications: *Chablis Grand Cru*: The seven top
vineyards
Chablis Premier Cru: The next 12 best vineyards
Petit Chablis: Now usually just sold as AC Chablis.

Regions and Styles: *Reds*: *Bourgogne Coulanges-
la-Vineuse*: Rare, light, delicate Pinot Noir (B).
Bourgogne Epineuil: Small quantities of light,
fragrant reds (B)
Bourgogne Irancy: The best-known Chablis red,
made from Pinot Noir with a little Csar. Light,
perfumed, fresh and fruity. Best young but it will
age (B).

PRODUCE OF FRANCE
CLIGNET ®

MISE EN BOUTEILLES EN FRANCE

MUSCADET
DE SÈVRE & MAINE

70 cl ℮
11% VOL

APPELLATION MUSCADET DE SÈVRE ET MAINE CONTROLÉE
MIS EN BOUTEILLE PAR FRANÇOIS DE CLIGNET
Ⓡ N° 048   NÉGOCIANT A VERTOU (LOIRE-ATLANTIQUE)

Whites: *Chablis*: Dry, green, steely, and made to be
drunk young. (1).
Petit Chablis: An AOC, but most growers prefer to
sell it as Chablis (1).
Grand Cru Chablis: Expensive but frequently superb
and more complex than Chablis. Needs many years
to develop full depth of flavour (1).
Premier Cru Chablis: More complex than Chablis,
but without depth of flavour or longevity as Grand
Cru (1).
Sauvignon de St. Bris: An excellent Sauvignon:
fresh, crisp and green with flavours of gooseberry
and a bone dry finish (1).

Best recent vintages: 1989, 1988, 1986, 1985,
1983, 1978.

BEAUJOLAIS
The most southerly region of Burgundy, running to
the west of the N6 motorway from the southern
limits of the Macon to the suburbs of Lyon.
Although only 30 miles by nine miles, it is one of
France's largest wine producing regions. More than
9,500 wine-makers produce an average 150 millions
bottles a year from 55,000 acres of vineyards.

Grapes: *Gamay* for the reds, a little white is made from *Chardonnay*.

Classification: *Beaujolais*: Any red or white from the region. Best drunk young
Beaujolais Supérieur: As above but one degree more alcohol. Tends to travel better.
Beaujolais Nouveau: A third of the harvest is sold as new wine in November, only two months after the grapes have been picked. Maceration Carbonique is used to produce this fresh, fun wine. The grapes are not pressed but placed in vats, where those at the bottom are crushed by the weight of those above. This starts fermentation resulting in a deep coloured, very fruity wine with low tannin and high acidity, ideal for drinking young.
Beaujolais Rosé: Can be excellent, fresh, crisp and fruity.
Beaujolais Villages: One of the 39 villages, mostly in the north, producing wines with more body and fruit. The wine is released in the spring following the harvest. Can be aged.
Beaujolais Crus: Ten communes producing the region's best wine which is full bodied and fruity. In good years this wine has great ageing potential. The Crus are: Brouilly, Chénas, Chiroubles, Côte de Brouilly, Fleurie, Juliénas, Morgon, Moulin-à-Vent, Régnié and St. Amour. Can be aged.

Tasting notes: Most Beaujolais is light, fruity, thirst-quenching and made to drink young and chilled, although the Nouveau improves no end if left until Christmas, or Easter in very good years. Only the Crus, full bodied and full of flavour, are made to last, and Morgan, Chénas and Moulin-à-Vent particularly can be kept for many years.

Best recent vintages: 86 good, 87 very good, 88 good, 89 very good for Villages and Crus.

CHAMPAGNE

When asked why he drank Champagne for breakfast every morning, Nöel Coward replied, 'Doesn't everyone?'.

'In victory you deserve it; in defeat you need it,' said Napoleon.

Champagne is the most northerly vineyard in France, a large plain split by the River Marne 90 miles east of Paris. There are about 72,000 acres of vineyards within the Champagne appellation, some 15,000 growers, more than 4,500 producers including 110 Houses and about 250 miles of tunnels for storing and ageing the wine. Annual sales are around 250 million bottles, of which 40 per cent is exported. The UK is the biggest export market followed by the United States.

Champagne, the world's finest sparkling wine, comes from one of four vine growing areas – Montagne de Reims, Vallée de la Marne, Côte des Blancs and Aube – and the wine must be at least one year old to be sold as non-vintage, and three years old for vintage.

Champagne is produced by two fermentations, the first in tanks or barrels and the second in the bottle in which it is sold. After the first fermentation, wines from as many as 30 or 40 different vineyards are selected to produce the Cuvée (blend). Non vintage wines can contain wines from different vintages, while for a Vintage, only wine from a single year is allowed.

It is the second fermentation, the *méthode champenoise*, which converts the still wine into sparkling because gases produced when sugar is converted to alcohol are trapped inside the bottle.

The wine is then put in a rack and given a little twist every day until the neck points towards the ground. This action – *remuage* – moves all the sediment into the neck from where it is disgorged. The level is then topped up and the bottled corked.

Bottle sizes:

Magnum	equivalent to	2 bottles
Jeroboam	equivalent to	4 bottles
Rehoboam	equivalent to	6 bottles
Methuselah	equivalent to	8 bottles
Salmanazar	equivalent to	12 bottles
Balthazar	equivalent to	16 bottles
Nebuchadnezzar	equivalent to	20 bottles

Grapes: *Chardonnay*: For elegance, richness, perfume, depth and longevity.
Pinot Noir: For body and depth of flavour.
Pinot Meunier: For softness and fruit.

Styles: *Blanc de Blanc*: Made only from Chardonnay. Light, fresh and creamy (1).
Blanc de Noirs: Made only from lightly pressed Pinot grapes. Golden-yellow coloured, heavy and fruity. Needs time to develop elegance (1).
Brut: Very dry (1).
Crémant: Made with less pressure so it has smaller bubbles. Creamy (1).
Cuvée de Prestige: Expensive, top of the range, usually vintage and often in extravagant bottles (1).
Demi-Sec: Medium sweet to sweet (6).
Doux: Very sweet, rich dessert Champagne (8).
Extra Dry: Not as dry as Brut, and not to be confused with Extra Brut (2).
Grande Marque: Used by the top Houses in Champagne.
Non-Dosage: No added sweetness. Bone dry (1).
Non-Vintage: The ordinary Cuvée blended to provide consistency each year.
Récemment Dégorgé: Champagne disgorged much later than usual and sold almost immediately. Elegant, balanced, mature wine (1).
Rosé: Pink Champagne, full of flavour and berry fruit. Drink young (1).
Sec: Slightly sweet (2).

Vintage: A Cuvée from a single year. Classier wines that age well. Must be at least three years old but are often much older (1).

A new code, agreed in 1990, offers the following label information:
NM: A Champagne House.
CM: Champagne made by a co-operative.
RM: Grower producing Champagne from his own grapes.
RC: A grower selling Champagne produced by a co-operative.
SR: A company created by wine growers who are all members of the same family.
MA: Buyer's Own Brand.

Other wines from Champagne: *Coteaux Champenois*: Expensive still red, rosé or white produced with their own AOC. The most famous red is Bouzy which is light and matures quickly although some age well (B). They all tend to be acidic.
Rosé des Riceys: Made only in certain years from ripe Pinot Noir, with incredible colour – 'red sky at sunset' – and austere, gooseberry flavour. Expensive (1).
Champagne is sold ready for drinking but many can be kept for 4–5 years if stored correctly in a cool, dark place. Vintages can be kept much longer.

Vintages: were declared in 1985 (exceptional), 1983, 1982, 1981, 1980.

LOIRE
The Loire is France's longest river, flowing almost 650 miles from the foothills of the Massif Central in the Ardèche to the Atlantic Ocean west of Nantes. Fairy tale castles overlook the vineyards that flank most of the river and its tributaries. Near its source are the vineyards of Sancerre, Pouilly and the Côteaux du Giennois. Reuilly and Quincy mingle among the southern tributaries. To the east of Tours is Vouvray, and then Chinon, Bourgueil, Saumur, Muscadet and a scattering of smaller appellations as you near the sea.

Red and Rosé wines: Grapes: *Cabernet Franc*:
Produces the best reds (Chinon, Touraine and
Anjou) from light and fruity to full bodied, with
great depth and longevity.
Cabernet Sauvignon: Mostly grown for blending.
Gamay: Produces light, fruity wines, red and rosé,
but not as good as Beaujolais.
Groslot: For the local light and fruity rosé, which is
drunk in cafés and bars.
Pinot Noir: Grown mainly for red Sancerre.

Regions and Styles: *Anjou Rouge*: Light, earthy
and fruity, drink youngish (B).
Anjou Rouge Gamay: Very drinkable, light and
fruity (A).
Anjou Villages: A new AC covering the best reds.
Drink youngish (B).
Bourgueil: Slightly harsh and earthy when young
but mature into refreshing, fruity, sharp wines (B).
Cabernet d'Anjou: Upmarket rosé, dryish and full
of fruit and flavour (B).
Chinon: Full flavour of currants and berries, ripe,
earthy red, a hint of violets. Fun when young but
ages well (B).

Rosé d'Anjou: Can be light, fresh and fruity but often lacks fruit (A).

Rosé de Loire: Dryish and fruity. Drink young (B).

Sancerre Rouge: Light-bodied, but the best are fragrant and full of fruit (B).

Saumur Rouge: Pleasant, fruity and refreshing when young. Softens, mellows and develops more body (B).

Saumur-Champigny: Better than the above, with more intense fruit (B).

St. Nicolas de Bourgueil: Light, earthy and usually better than Bourgueil (B).

Touraine: Easy drinking, light, fruity reds. Drink young and chilled (A).

White Wines: Grapes: *Chardonnay*: Becoming more popular, especially in Haut-Poitou.

Chenin Blanc: The main white variety in Anjou. High in acidity and sugar when ripe, produces good crisp, fresh peachy whites, still and sparkling, and delicious long lasting dessert wines.

Melon de Bourgogne (Muscadet): Low acidity, youthful, light, easy-drinking wine.

Sauvignon Blanc: For Pouilly, Sancerre and Touraine, for aromatic, dry, sharp, grassy, fruity thirst quenchers.

Regions and Styles: *Anjou Blanc*: Dry, easy drinking, earthy flavours and hints of honeysuckle (2).

Bonnezeaux: Soft and fruity, sweet whites. Age well (8).

Coteaux de L'Aubance: Mostly light, fruity and medium sweet. Will age (5).

Coteaux du Layon: Good value, medium sweet to sweet, honeyed, nutty and long lasting (5/8).

Crémant de Loire: Soft, balanced sparkling wine. Drink young (2).

Gros Plant: Local grape producing light, very sharp wine. Drink young and ideally with seafood (1).

Menetou-Salon: Light, fruity, flowery, aromatic Sauvignon best drunk young (1).

Montlouis: Dry and sweet wines. Fruity and with great longevity (1/8).

Muscadet: Dry and crisp with high acidity. Needs good fruit for balance. Drink young (1).
Muscadet de Sèvre-et-Maine: The best Muscadets. Bigger, nutty and creamy (1).
Muscadet des Côteaux de la Loire: Somewhere between the two above (1).
Muscadet sur lie: Muscadet held on the lees for more freshness, fruit and flavour (1).
Pouilly-Fumé: Classy, smoky, fruity, flinty and dry. Drink youngish (1).
Pouilly sur Loire: Best drunk locally with food. Made from Chasselas (1).
Quarts de Chaume: Expensive but magnificent, long lasting, luscious desserts (8).
Quincy: Dry Sancerre-style but cheaper. Drink young (1).
Reuilly: Light and fruity, often austere. Drink young (1).
Sancerre: At its best crisp, fragrant, fresh and full of flavour (gooseberries). Drink young (1).
Saumur: Méthode champenoise, refreshing, crisp and acidic. Drink young (1).
Savennières: Dry and dull when young, but honeyed and rounded when aged (1/7).

Touraine: Aromatic and fruity, crisp and grassy.
Drink young (1).
Vouvray: Still and sparkling from dry to sweet.
Young wines appear dry because of high acidity, but
they become honeyed and rounded with age (1/7).

RHÔNE
The vineyards of the Rhône extend from just below
Lyon as far south as Avignon straddling both sides of
the river but not continuously. In the north, the
vineyard belt is rarely more than a few hundred yards
wide, while in the south the vineyards stretch out
into the widening valleys.
The northern vineyards are hot and rocky and all the
famous red wines are produced from the Syrah
grape, while in the south where many of the wines
are blended there have been enormous
improvements in the past few years.

Red wines: **Grapes**: *Carignan*: Produces large crops
of big, heady table and dessert wines. Ages well.
Cinsaut: Produces light wines and adds warmth and
fullness in blends.
Grenache: The main grape in Southern Rhône. High
alcohol, good fruit and hints of pepper. Used in red,
rosé and dessert wine.
Syrah: Produces wines of enormous depth, fruitiness
and longevity.
Viognier: Although this is a white variety, a little is
blended in with Côte Rôtie to add fragrance.

Regions and Styles: *Châteauneuf-du-Pape*: Big,
powerful, warm and fruity, this wine needs years to
develop fully (D).
Cornas: Big, powerful and jammy. Not as complex
or refined as Hermitage. Needs ageing (D).
Coteaux du Tricastin: Soft, refreshing, peppery and
fruity. Usually blended, and best drunk young.
although the best wines age well (B).
Côte-Rôtie: Rich, ripe, complex, aromatic wines that
will last decades (D).
Côtes du Lubéron: A new AC: light, fruity and
perfumed. Drink young/youngish (B).

```
CHAMPAGNE
BRUT

DUPONT ᴇᴛ DURAND
CUVÉE SÉLECTIONNÉE

75 cl                                          12% vol.
Elaboré par Société Dupont et Durand, 51100 Reims, France
NM-204-007
```

Côtes du Rhône: Deep coloured and fruity with a spicy nose. Full-bodied and best drunk young (C).
Côtes du Rhône Villages: More body and fruit than the above, this wine can age well (C).
Côtes du Ventoux: Like Côtes du Rhône but lighter, fruity and easy drinking. Drink young (C).
Crozes-Hermitage: Big, full and fruity. Age well. Lack the finesse of Hermitage (D).
Gigondas: Big, plummy fruity, flavoursome wines (D).
Hermitage: Rich, fruity and warming with hints of violets and great longevity (D).
Lirac: Good value, medium bodied and fruity. Will age well (C).
St.Joseph: Firm, fruity and tannic. Need time to soften (C7.
Tavel: One of France's best rosé wines. Strong, full and fruity. Needs three or four years to be at its best (A).

White wines: Grapes: *Clairette*: Light in fruit and flavour. Makes still and sparkling wines.
Grenache Blanc: Produces low acid, soft, fruity wines. Must be drunk young.

Marsanne: Produces big, rich, fat long lasting wines
with complex flavours.
Muscat: Usually blended to add aroma and grapey
flavour.
Roussanne: Produces fine, fragrant delicate wines.
Ugni Blanc: Produces light, crisp, refreshing wines
which are best drunk young.
Viognier: Produces elegant, dry wines, with rich
bouquets and lush flavours.

Regions and Styles: *Château Grillet*: The smallest
AC in France and therefore expensive. Uses Viognier
to produce delicate, dry but full flavoured whites,
which will age (2).
Châteauneuf-du-Pape: Powerful, rich, crisp, full
bodied and dry. Drink young (2).
Clairette de Die: Dull still wines, but a good value
methode champenoise sparkling wine. Drink
young (2).
Clairette de Die Tradition: Single fermentation
sparkling wine which is peachy and delicious when
very young (2).
Condrieu: Powerful floral bouquets. Dry, fat and
fruity. Age well (3).
Coteaux du Tricastin: Dry, fresh and fruity. Must be
drunk young (2).
Côtes du Lubéron: Fragrant, fruity wines, especially
when a little Chardonnay has been added. Drink
young (2).
Côtes du Rhône Blanc: Good, refreshing, fruity
quaffing wines. Drink young (2).
Côtes du Rhône Villages: Better quality than the
above, but still to be drink young (2).
Crozes-Hermitage: Dry, fresh and fruity with good
acidity. Age well (2).
Hermitage: Dry, big, full, rich and fruity when
young. Full bodied and powerful with complex
bouquets and greatness when aged (3).
Lirac: Dry and fragrant but can lack zest (2).
St.Joseph: Not common, dry, crisp and nutty. Drink
young (2).
St.Péray: Indifferent table wine and drinkable but
unexciting sparkler (2).

Fortified wines: *Muscat de Beaumes de Venise*:
Wonderful, fresh and honeyed, with a big rich
bouquet (8).
Rasteau: Red, white and rosé. Big, sweet, strong and
grapey (8).

OTHER REGIONS OF FRANCE:
SAVOIE AND JURA
Savoie is close to the Swiss border, a few miles south
of Geneva and most of its production is white wine,
although it does produce light red and rosé.
The Jura vineyards start about 25 miles north west of
Geneva and, like Savoie, cover about 3,000 acres.
Red, white, rosé and sparkling wines are produced,
as well as the unusual Vin de Paille, so-named
because the grapes are dried on straw before pressing
to impart very special characteristics.

Grapes (Savoie): *Chasselas*: Light and fruity but
must be drunk young.
Altesse: Rich and fragrant.
Jacquère: Dry, sharp and fruity.
Chardonnay: Elegant, light, dry and crisp.
Mondeuse: Big, plummy and rich.
Gamay: Soft, perfumed, fruity.
Pinot Noir: light and fruity, with depth.

Grapes (Jura): *Savagnin*: Develops enormous
complexity and flavours when old – the best time to
drink it.
Trousseau: Makes light, elegant, fruity reds.
Poulsard: For dry, fruity, perfumed rosé.

Styles: *Red*: *Arbois (Jura)*: Light, but rich in
flavour. Will age (B).
Côtes de Jura: As above. Good value, light and fruity
(B).
Vin de Savoie: Usually blended, light and fruity,
Drink young (B).
White: *Arbois* (Jura): light, fresh, and fragrant,
especially if Chardonnay added. Drink young (2).
Bugey (Savoie): Very good, light, fresh, crisp and
fruity Chardonnay. Drink young (2).

Cérpy (Savoie): Light, dry, fruity and floral. Drink very young (2).

L'Etoile (Jura): Light, aromatic, dry, crisp and herby. Drink young (2).

Roussette de Savoie: Usually blended, dry, crisp and full of fruit. Drink young (2).

Seyssel (Savoie): Fragrant, refreshing stills and elegant dry sparkling wines, (mousseux). Both need drinking young (2).

Vin Jaune (Jura): An acquired taste. Big, rich, strong and immensely long living. Rare (3).

Vin de Paille (Jura): Golden, very sweet with rich, nutty flavour and dry finish. Improve with ageing 50 years or more (8).

Vin de Savoie: Good value. Crisp, dry and full of fruit. Drink young (2).

MIDI AND PROVENCE

The Midi is a huge wine producing region stretching from the Rhône estuary westwards to the Spanish border, and includes the Languedoc-Roussillon and a host of small communes producing good value, everyday table wines. Quality improves year by year and there are some exceptional vineyards. Most wine is blended.

Grapes: *Ugni Blanc.*
Clairette.
Macabeo.
Chardonnay.
Sémillon.
Sauvignon Blanc.
Carignan.
Cinsault.
Grenache.
Syrah.
Mourvèdre.
Cabernet Sauvignon.

Styles: *Red and Rosé*: *Bandol*: Deep colour, big bouquet, soft, spicy and plummy fruit. Age well (C).
Bellet: Medium-bodied with a perfumed bouquet and rich berry fruit. Drink youngish (B).
Cassis: Big, solid reds best drunk young. Light fruity rosé (C).
Collioure: Big, powerful wines which are intensely fruity. Age well (D).
Corbiéres: Soft and fruity with a spicy, fruity bouquet. Drink youngish (B).
Costières du Gard: Light, fruity and easy drinking. Drink youngish (B).
Coteaux d'Aix-en-Provence: A new AC. Light, plummy and fruity. Age well (B).
Coteaux des Baux-en-Provence: Soft, rich and fruity. Age well (B).
Coteaux du Languedoc: Big and fruity for every day drinking. Drink young (B).
Coteaux Varois: New VDQS. Decent, good value everyday fruity reds (C).
Côtes de Provence: A wide range of fruity, spicy reds which can age well (C).
Côtes du Roussillon: Soft and fruity, with a good nose and a touch of spice. Drink young (B).
Côtes du Roussillon Villages: Good value and fruity. Have finesse. Can age (B).

Faugères: Big, fruity, warming, spicy country wines. Age well (C).
Fitou: Big, soft, spicy and fruity. Drink youngish (C).
Minervois: Big, rich berry fruit with hints of pepper. Drink young (C).
Palette: Rare, rich, fruity and medium-bodied. Age well (B).
St. Chinian: Light, medium-bodied, fruity and elegant. Drink young (B).
Vin de Pays de L'Hérault: Medium- to full-bodied, fruity and strong. Drink young (C).
Vin de Pays des Bouches du Rhône: Good value, everyday big and fruity (C).
Vin de Pays du Gard: Ever-improving, soft, big and fruity. Can age well (C).
White: *Bandol*: Crisp, fresh and fragrant. Drink young (2).
Bellet: Classy and fragrant with surprising depth. Drink youngish (3).
Cassis: Dry, herby whites. Can be light on fruit. Drink young (2).
Clairette de Bellegarde: Dry, and often disappointing. Drink young (2).

SOUTH WEST

A massive wine producing area running from Bergerac to the west of Bordeaux, and stretching south to the Spanish frontier and south east to the Mediterranean.

Grapes: *Sauvignon Blanc.*
Sémillon.
Muscadelle.
Cabernet Sauvignon.
Cabernet Franc.
Merlot.
Malbec.

Styles: *Red*: *Béarn*: Light, fresh and fruity. Drink youngish (A).
Bergerac: Light, elegant and rich with concentrated fruit. Drink youngish (C).

Cahors: New, softer style with rich, plummy fruit. Very long lasting (C).

Côtes de Bergerac: Bigger and with more fruit than Bergerac. Age well (C).

Côtes de Buzet: Good and classy, with Cabernet Sauvignon curranty fruit. Age well (C).

Cîtes de Duras: Light, fruity Bordeaux type wine (C).

Côtes de Saint-Mont: Medium-bodied, soft, fruity and full flavoured. Drink youngish (C).

Côtes du Frontonnais: Very soft, fruity and plummy. Drink youngish (C).

Côtes du Marmandais: Easy-drinking, soft, fruity wines. Drink youngish (B).

Gaillac: Light, fresh and fruity. Made to drink young (B).

Irouléguy: Big, rich, earthy and strong. Age well (D).

Madiran: Big, rich and chewy. Needs ageing to mellow it (D).

Pécharmant: Intense flavour and fruit. High in tannin. Age well (C).

Vin de Lavillediu: Medium-bodied, fresh and fruity. Drink youngish (C).

White: Bergerac sec: Dry, fruity, grassy, Bordeaux-style wine. Drink young (1).

Blanquette de Limoux: Fine, dry, crisp, grassy and sparkling. Can age well (1).

Côtes de Bergerac Moelleux: Soft, fat and fruity, medium sweet / sweet. Can age well (6 / 8).

Côtes de Duras: Fresh, dry, crisp and fruity (1).

Côtes de Saint Mont: Soft, fresh and fruity. Drink young (1).

Côtes du Marmandais: Soft, dry, full flavoured. Drink young (2).

Gaillac: Light, dry, fresh and fruity. Also produces good honeyed sparklers (2 / 8).

Irouléguy: Light and dry but often lacking fruit (2).

Jurancon: Dry, tangy and full of flavour; or sweet, honeyed and peachy and long lasting (1 / 8).

Monbazillac: Luscious, rich and classy. Age well (7).

Montravel: Dry, crisp and fruity. Drink young (1).

Pacheron du Vic-Bilh: Bursting with aromas and flavours. Dry to sweet (2-7).

Pineau de Charente: Strong and sweet. Drink young and chilled. Good aperitif (7).

Rosette: Soft, sweet and full of flavour. Drink youngish (7).

Tursan: Full-bodied and rich. Drink youngish (3).

Vin de Pays Charentais: Clean, crisp, fresh and fruity. Drink young (1).

Vin de Pays des Côtes de Gascogne: Good value, big, dry and full of fruit and flavour. Drink young (1).

CORSICA

Frequently left out of wine guides, Corsica produces lots of good, honest everyday drinking wine. Quality has improved considerably and some vineyards now have very good potential.

Grapes: *Vermentino*.
Ugni Blanc.
Barbarossa.
Nielluccio.
Sciacarello.
Carignan.
Cinsault.
Grenache.

Styles:	*Ajaccio*:	*red* – medium-bodied and fruity with a good bouquet. Drink young (D).
		white – dry, crisp and fruity, good acidity. Drink young (2).
	Patrimonio:	*red* – big, full bodied, rich and fruity, age well (C).
		white – light, dry, fragrant, stylish (2).
	Vin de Corse:	*red* – big, rich, strong, ripe fruit, drink youngish (D).
		white – fresh and fruity, drink young (3).

VINS DE PAYS: Since the introduction of the Vins de Pays classification in 1973, 144 different varieties have qualified for the appellation in one of the three categories – Z (Zonal), D (Departement) and R (Regional).
These wines are not expensive and many have made tremendous strides in recent years, You can afford to experiment with them. Generally the reds are better than the whites.

The full list of Vins de Pays is:

l'Agenais	Z
l'Ain	D
d'Allobrogie	Z
des Alpes de Haute Provence	D
de l'Ardailhou	Z
de l'Ardeche	D
d'Argens	Z
de l'Aude	D
de l'Aveyron	D
des Balmes Dauphinoises	Z
du Bas Rhin	D
de la Benovie	Z
du Berange	Z
de Bessan	Z
de Bigorre	Z
des Bouches-du-Rhone	D
du Bourbonnais	Z
de Cassan	Z
Catalan	Z
de Caux	Z
de Cessenon	Z
de la Charente	D
Charentais	Z
du Cher	D
de la Cité de Carcassonne	Z
des Collines de la Moure	Z
des Collines Rhodaniennes	Z
du Comite de Grignan	Z
des Comites Rhodaniens	R
du Comite Tolosan	R
de la Côte d'Or	D
des Coteaux de Bessilles	Z
des Coteaux Cevenols	Z
des Coteaux Charitois	Z
des Coteaux de Ceze	Z
de Coteaux de Coiffy	Z
des Coteaux de Fontcaude	Z
des Coteaux de Glanes	Z
des Coteaux de la Cabrerisse	Z
des Coteaux de l'Ardeche	Z
des Coteaux de Laurens	Z
des Coteaux de Miramont	Z
des Coteaux de Murviel	Z
des Coteaux de Narbonne	Z
des Coteaux d'Enserune	Z
des Coteaux de Peyriac	Z
des Coteaux des Baronnies	Z
des Coteaux des Fenouilledes	Z
des Coteaux du Cher et de l'Arnon	Z
des Coteaux de Gresivaudan	Z
des Coiteaux du Lezignanais	Z
des Coteaux du Libron	Z
des Coteaux Littoral Audois	Z
des Coteaux du Pont du Gard	Z
des Coteaux du Quercy	Z
des Coteaux du Salagou	Z
des Coteaux du Salaves	Z
des Coteaux du Termenes	Z
des Coteaux et Terrasses de Montauban	Z
des Coteaux Flaviens	Z
des Côtes Catalanes	Z
des Côtes de Gascogne	Z
des Côtes de Lastours	Z

des Côtes de Libac	Z	du Maine-et-Loire	D
des Côtes de Montestruc	Z	des Marches de	
des Côtes de Perignan	Z	Bretagne	Z
des Côtes de Prouille	Z	des Maures	Z
des Côtes de Thau	Z	de la Meuse	D
des Côtes de Thongue	Z	du Mont Baudile	Z
des Côtes du Brian	Z	du Mont Bouquet	Z
des Côtes du Ceressou	Z	du Mont Caume	Z
des Côtes du		des Monts de la Grage	Z
Condomois	Z	d'Oc	R
des Côtes du Tarn	Z	de Petite Crau	Z
des Côtes du Vidourle	Z	de Pezenas	Z
de la Côte Vermeille	Z	de la Principaute	
de Cucugnan	Z	d'Orange	Z
des Deux-Sevres	D	du Puy-de-Dome	D
de Dordogne	D	des Pyrenees-	
de la Drome	D	Atlantiques	D
de Franche Comte	Z	des Pyrenees-	
du Gard	D	Orientales	D
du Gers	D	de Retz	Z
de la Gironde	D	des Sables du Golfe	
des Gorges de		du Lion	Z
l'Herault	Z	de Saint-Sardos	Z
des Gorges et Côtes		de la Sarthe	D
de Millau	Z	du Tarn	D
des Hautes-Alpes	D	du Tarn-et-Garonne	D
des Haute-Garonne	D	des Terroirs Landais	Z
de Huaterive en Pays		de Thezac-Perricard	Z
d'Aude	Z	du Torgan	Z
de la Haute-Vallee		d'Urfe	Z
de l'Aude	Z	de l'Uzege	Z
de la Haute-Vallee		du Val-de-Cesse	Z
de l'Orb	Z	du Val-de-Dagne	Z
des Hauts de Badens	Z	du Val de Montferrand	Z
de l'herault	D	du Val d'Orbieu	Z
de l'Ile de Beaute	Z	de la Vallee du Paradis	Z
de l'Indre	D	des Vals d'Agly	Z
de l'Indre-et-Loire	D	du Var	D
de l'Isere	D	du Vaucluse	D
de Jardin de la France	R	de la Vaunage	Z
des Landes	D	de la Vendee	D
de la Loire-Atlantique	D	de la Vicomte	
du Loiret	D	d'Aumelas	Z
du Loir-et-Cher	D	de la Vienne	D
du Lot	D	de la Vistrenque	Z
du Lot-et-Garonne	D	de l'Yonne	D

Germany

History: The Romans planted the first vineyards and have had the greatest impact on German wine-making. The Rhine was a natural 'highway' and when settlements sprang up along its banks, vineyards quickly followed. For many centuries inheritance legislation, based on Roman laws, obliged estates to be equally divided among descendants and so vineyards became smaller and smaller. The exceptions to this were the great estates owned by the Church, especially in the Rhine and Palatinate. If you visit the wineries of these old estates you can see from the size of the massive presses, often operated by teams of oxen, just how big the enterprises were. The size of the barrels is another indicator. The world's largest wine barrel is in the Friedrichsbahn cellars in Heidelberg and holds 185,500 litres. The massive acreage of Church-owned vineyards were given to the State in 1803 by Napoleon, and the State is still the largest single vineyard owner.

Current situation: Germany has about 250,000 acres of vineyards, less than 1 per cent of the world's total; yet the 85,000 producers account for more than 12 per cent of global wine production. In 1971, new wine lines were introduced with quality determined by sweetness: the sweeter the wine, the higher the quality. The wine laws do not limit quantity produced as most other countries do, which explains why Germany produces so much wine and why the quality level on the label does not always match the quality in the bottle.

That said, however, Germany does produce some of the world's finest wines, from steely dry to honeyed sweet, with enormous longevity. While still only a minority taste, the excellent new style dry (*trocken*) and half-dry (*halbtrocken*) wines show that the best German wine-makers are capable of. There are also excellent sparkling (*sekt*) wines. The worst thing about German wines is the wine language, but it is worth getting to know the tongue-twisting classifications. Britain is by far Germany's largest export market, followed by the United States.

Classifications: (*Deutscher Tafelwein*: Table wine from anywhere in Germany. Quality varies enormously. Big retailers' own label can be very drinkable. Do not confuse with ECT Tafelweins, which are Europe-wide blends of low quality.
Landwein: A new category of dry (trocken) or half-dry (halbtrocken) wines similar to the French *vin de pays*. Must come from one of 15 designated areas.
Qualitätswein bestimmter Anbaugebiete (QbA): Wine from 11 designated areas, which must be made from approved grape varieties. Each bottle carries a batch number (*Amtliche Prüfnummer* or AP) as proof that it complies with QbA status. Sugar can be added to increase sweetness. Best drunk young.
The QbA areas are: Ahr, Baden, Franken, Hessische Bergstrasse, Mittelrhein, Mosel-Saar-Ruwer, Nahe, Rheingau, Rheinhessen, Rheinpfalz and Württemberg.
Qualitätswein mit Prädikat (QmP):
The six quality gradings, calculated on level of

natural sweetness in the grape at picking. Extra sugar cannot be added.

The quality grades are:

Kabinett: Light, fruity and delicate, usually dry.

Spätlese: Late-picked grapes for higher natural sugar content. Dry to sweet.

Auslese: Late-picked and selected grapes only. Rich and sweet.

Beerenauslese: Selected grapes affected by 'noble rot', which increases sugar levels. Always sweet and luscious, high alcoholic strengh.

Trockenbeerenauslese: It's easier to say TBA. Made from raisin-like grapes which have shrivelled because of the noble rot. Strong, luscious, expensive.

Eiswein: Rare, made from grapes which have frozen on the vines. Intense sweetness.

More than 85 per cent of wine production is white. Reds have tended to be light, delicate and lacking fruit and tannin, but there have been improvements and there are now some very drinkable dry reds, especially from Baden and Württemberg.

Grapes: *Reds*: *Spätburgunder*: Light and fruity, with a touch of sweetness.

Portugieser: Light with low acidity and fruit. May be blended to soften high acidity.

Trollinger: (Württemberg only). Late-ripening, fragrant, fresh and fruity, with good acidity.

Whites: *Riesling*: 21 per cent of the total vineyard area. Produces almost all the finest wine from racy, steely dry to lusciously sweet. Bouquet and depth of flavour intensifies according to ripeness, and the very sweet wines, some of the world's best, have great longevity.

Müller-Thurgau: 24 per cent of the total vineyard area. Prolific, early-ripening, flowery bouquet, with good fruit.

Silvaner: Prolific, early-ripening, earthily fruity, mellow and honeyed when aged.

Many other white varieties are grown including *Gewürztraminer*, *Huxelrebe*, *Kerner*, *Morio-Muskat*, *Rülander*, and *Scheurebe*.

Regions: ther are 11 wine-producing regions
(*bestimmte Anbaugebiete*), which are divided into
34 sub-regions (*Bereich*). These are again divided
into villages (*Gemeinden*) and then into individual
estates or vineyards (*Einzellagen*), '*Grosslage*' on a
label indicates the wine is from a number of growers,
all producing the same style. The group may be
drawn from a wide area despite the fact that the
name appears after Einzellagen. Most regions have
some *sekt* production.

Ahr

Germany's second-smallest wine region with about
1,000 acres of vines straddling the Ahr, a tributary of
the Rhine flowing south of Bonn in the north-west of
the country. About 70 per cent of the wine is red,
usually blended, or single-varietal rosé (*weissherbst*),
made from either the Spätburgunder or Portugieser,
and 30 per cent white.

Styles: *Portugeiser*: Very light and fruity. Must be
drunk young if dry. Sweeter wines will age (A/B).
Müller Thurgau: Flowery, light and lively. Drink
young (3).
Reds: Often blended. Light, fruity, drink young
(A).
Riesling: Aromatic, fresh, crisp and sharp. Ages well
(2).
Spätburgunder: Light and soft, with a delicate
bouquet. Can have velvety fruit (B).
Weissherbsdt: Usually made from 100 per cent
Spätburgunder. Soft, warm and fruity.
Traditionally, the rosé was medium-sweet to sweet.
The tendency now is towards a dryer style, but there
are some very good Ausleses which age well (2/7).

Baden

A sprawling area of about 35,000 acres of vineyards
in south-west Germany. About 75 per cent of
production is white and 25 per cent red and rosé,
making it the second largest area in Germany for
reds.

Styles: *Gutedel*: Dry, light, very drinkable. Drink young (3).
Müller-Thurgau: Aromatic, light, fruity and refreshing. Drink young (4).
Riesling: Clean, crisp, spicy, refreshing and fruity. Age well (3).
Ruländer: Big, rich, fruity and full-bodies. Age well (2).
Silvaner: Light and delicate. Drink young (4).
Spätburgunder: Very light, delicate and fruity. Drink young, though sweets age well (a).
Traminer: Light but flowery bouquet and delicate fruit. Drink young (3).
Weissherbst: Very light in colour, but full bodied and fruity. Dry to medium-sweet. Best drunk young (2/7).

Franken

A large, scattered area of vineyards in north-east Bavaria, centred around Würzburg, one of Germany's most famous beer-producing centres. Franken wines are bottled in the famous flasks known as *'Bocksbeutels'*. More than 75 per cent of production is white; the remainder red and rosé. Franken is noted for its dry wines, though many seem deceptively sweet.

Styles: *Müller-Thurgau*: Light and aromatic, but can lack fruit. Drink young (3).
Riesling: Big, crisp and fruity, with hints of peaches. Age well (3).
Rieslaner: A Riesling-Silvaner cross, which needs to ripen well. Produces crisp, fruity quality wines, which can age (3).
Scheurebe: Big, rich and spicy in good years. Age well (4).
Silvaner: Crisp, full-bodied, earthy and good depth of fruit. Drink young (3).

Hessische Bergstrasse

The smallest of Germany's wine regions lies east of the Rhein and north of Heidelberg. There are less than 1,000 acres of vine and virtually all production is white. The wines are noted for their fruitiness and earthy acidity.

Styles: *Gewürztraminer*: In good years can be elegant, fresh and fruity. Will age (3).
Müller Thurgau: Big aromatic nose. Light in body and fruity. Drink young (3).
Riesling: Fresh and fruity, with good acidity. Mostly drunk young but will age (3).
Silvaner: Light-bodied, fresh, fruity and earthy. Drink young (3).

Mittelrhein

The vineyards stretch for about 10 miles south from Bonn to Bingen. There are about 1,800 acres of vineyards and almost all production is white – about two per cent is red, including the Spätburgunder Drachenblut (Dragon's Blood). In German folklore, it was here that Siegfried slew the dragon. The vineyards produce many excellent but underrated wines so there are bargains.

Styles: *Müller Thurgau*: Light and fruity, but lacks real depth. Drink young (3).
Riesling: Sharp, very flowery, crisp and fruity. Age well in good years (3).
Spätburgunder: Stylish, light and fruity reds. Drink young (B).

1989
SCHLOSS SAARSTEIN

RIESLING

Mosel Saar Ruwer · Qualitätswein · trocken
Erzeugerabfüllung · D - 5512 Serrig
A. P. Nr. 3555014290 · Alc. 10.5% vol. · 750 ml

Mosel-Saar-Ruwer

More than 28,000 acres of vineyards which run
alongside the River Mosel as it runs south-west from
Koblenz to the French border. The Saar and Ruwer
are two tributaries which join the Mosel in the south.
All the production is white and the area makes some
of Germany's finest Rieslings.

Styles: *Elbling*: An old variety, producing classy
high-alcohol, sharp, still wine which must be drunk
young. A lively sekt (3/6).
Müller Thurgau: Aramatic and fruity, but a poor
second to Riesling. Drink young (3).
Riesling: Fresh, crisp, spicy, elegant and aromatic,
with good acidity and fruit. Age well. Ruwer
Riesling tends to be lighter and more elegant, with
great longevity, espcially for sweet wines. The Saar
Rieslings have more bite (3).

Nahe

About 12,000 acres of vines along the Nahe. A
tributary of the Rhein, from Bingen to Kirn

surrounding the town of Bad Kreuznach. Almost all production is white, with only two per cent red or rosé. The wines are noted for their light, elegant, perfumed style. They are soft and fresh, less acidic than the Rheingau and not as alcoholic as the Rheinpfalz. The region produces many fine Kabinett and Spätlese wines.

Styles: *Müller Thurgau*: Aromatic, medium- to full-bodied and fruity. Drink young (3).
Riesling: Classy and elegant, racy, soft, fruity and fragrant. Age well (3).
Silvaner: Aromatic, full-bodied and fruity. Drink young (3).

Rheingau

One of Germany's oldest wine regions, with about 6,750 acres of vines running north of the Rhein between Hochheim in the east and Lorch in the west. The vineyards face south to get maximum sun, and produce some of Germany's most wonderful Rieslings. The Rheingau is the home of Hoch, named after the village of Hochheim, which is traditionally sold in brown bottles. About 95 per cent of production is white, the rest red. Riesling is the main grape.

Styles: *Riesling*: Dry is fresh, perfumed, crisp and bursting with fruit. Best drunk young (3); sweet is luscious and honeyed, with great longevity (a).
Spätburgunder: Light, delicate and fruity. Drink young (B).

Rheinhessen

Germany's largest wine region with more than 65,000 acres below Mainz and to the west of the Rhein after it turns south at Wiesbaden. Best known as the largest producer of Liebfraumilch and the home of Blue Nun, although it produces many fine wines from several varieties. About 95 per cent of production is white, the rest red. Main varieties are Müller Thurgau and Silvaner although there is some Riesling, with small acreages of Portugieser and Spätburgunder for reds.

RUDOLF MÜLLER KG · WEINGUT · WEINKELLEREI · REIL/MOSEL

MOSEL - SAAR - RUWER
1975er
Reiler Mullay-Hofberg
Auslese
Riesling - Qualitätswein mit Prädikat
A. P. Nr. 2 598 176/34/76
Erzeugerabfüllung
WEINGUT

Rudolf Müller

0,7 L

Styles: *Müller Thurgau*: Light, soft, aromatic and flowery. Drink young (3).
Portugieser: Smooth, light and fruity. Drink young (3).
Riesling: Racy, spicy and acidic, with grapey fruit. Drink young (3).
Silvaner: Light, acidic, earthy and fruity. Drink young (3).
Spätburgunder: Can be elegant and light, with good fruit. Drink young (3).

Rheinpfalz

An area of 50,000 acres of vineyards, often called the Palatinate, which runs for 50 miles along the crest of the Haardt Mountains from just south of Worms to the French border and Alsace. Although it is Germany's second largest vineyard area it is often the biggest wine-producer. The northern half of the region as far south as Neustadt produces the best wines. The southern half has been extensively replanted and mechanised for production of the medium-sweet, perfumed wines so popular in Britain and the US. About 90 per cent of production is white. Much of it blended, and the remainder is red.

Styles: *Gewürztraminer*: Big, rich, fruity and spicy. Will age (3).

Kerner: Flowery, fragrant and well balanced. Drink young, but it will age (3).

Möller Thurgau: Light, aromatic and often lacking fruit. Drink young (3).

Portugieser: Very light and delicate but warming, with good fruit. Drink young (B).

Riesling: The best are spicy, full of fruit and flavour. Age well (3).

Spätburgunder: Light and soft with attractive fruit. Drink young (B).

Württemburg

Germany's biggest red wine producing region, although production is split almost evenly between red and white. It covers an area of about 24,000 acres of vineyard centred around Stuttgart and running south to Lake Constance.

Styles: *Müller Thurgau*: Light with a flowery bouquet and grapey fruit. Drink young (3).

Riesling: Fine, full-bodied, fresh and fruity. Drink young (3).

Schillerwein: The local rosé. Has body and good fruit. Drink young (4).

Spätburgunder: Medium-bodied, with good fruit and surprising depth (B).

Trollinger: Soft, light, fresh and grapey, with a hint of somkiness. Drink young (B).

Germany's fine wines have enormous longevity because of high residual sugar and acidity. The sweet wines can last for decades and develop fabulous complexity. Ageing in oak barriques also adds ageing potential and has improved some reds no end. Most of the wine, however, is made to drink young.

Best recent vintages: 1989, 1988, 1986, 1985, 1983, 1976.

Greece

History: An ancient wine making country as is often mentioned in classics such as the *Iliad* and *Odyssey*. Wine-making has changed little over the centuries and many of the techniques are similar to those used 2,000 years ago. Refugees from wine growing countries in the Balkans and Asia Minor who settled in Greece after the First World War rapidly expanded the vineyard acreage, and Greece was a significant exporter in the 1920s. Disease decimated the vineyards in the 1940s but forced a major replanting programme and much tougher disease control measures.

Current situation: There are about 400,000 acres of vineyard although these also produce table grapes and grapes for distillation wine. Today Greece produces about 550 million litres of wine a year and ranks 13th in the world production league. Most wine is cheap and cheerful, often sweet or resinated. The best-known wines are Retsina (flavoured with pine resin) and Demestica but whites are often oxidised and the reds old and heavy. A few producers, however, are waving the flag with light, fruity reds based on Cabernet, and heavier-bodied Italian-style reds; and good whites using Chardonnay and Sauvignon Blanc. The best of the sweet Muscats and Malvasias have always been worth drinking. Exports are steadily increasing.

Classification: Entry into the European Community encouraged moves towards some sort of quality system and there are now a number of designated appellations protecting individual wines or areas. The most exciting is the Côtes de Meliton.

Grapes: Local varieties predominate with Xynomavro and Tsantali the best red grapes, and Robola, Tsaoussi the best whites. The most promising results have come from blends of classical varieties, especially Cabernet Sauvignon, Chardonnay, Ugni Blanc and Sauvignon Blanc.

PRODUCT OF GREECE

ROBOLA *the original*

CEPHALONIAN

APPELLATION OF ORIGIN OF HIGH QUALITY

ΡΟΜΠΟΛΑ ΚΕΦΑΛΟΝΙΑΣ
ΟΝΟΜΑΣΙΑ ΠΡΟΕΛΕΥΣΕΩΣ ΑΝΩΤΕΡΑΣ ΠΟΙΟΤΗΤΟΣ

ΟΙΝΟΣ ΛΕΥΚΟΣ ΞΗΡΟΣ
ΠΑΡΑΓΩΓΗ – ΕΜΦΙΑΛΩΣΗ: ΑΓΡΟΤΟΒΙΟΜΗΧΑΝΙΚΟΣ
ΣΥΝΕΤΑΙΡΙΣΜΟΣ ΡΟΜΠΟΛΑΣ ΚΕΦΑΛΟΝΙΑΣ

DRY WHITE WINE
PRODUCED – BOTTLED BY: WINE PRODUCERS
COOPERATIVE CEPHALONIA – GREECE

e : 0,75 *lt*   ΟΙΝ ΒΑΣ 12% VOL

Regions: *Peleponnese*: This region has half the country's vineyards and produces a third of the wine. Patras is the main centre and produces clean, dry whites (2), sweet Muscats (8) and the luscious heady, sweet red dessert wine Mavrodaphne (8).
Attica: The second most productive region producing mostly white retsina, light rosé and red for the local tourist trade.
Macedonia: Produces promising reds and a good red Muscat. There are lots of new plantings, best wines are from the Côtes de Meliton, especially light, fruity, blended reds which age and develop well (C)
Rhodes: Produces mostly whites but the red Knight of Rhodes has AO status.
Samos: Most famous for its sweet Muscat of Samos.
Crete: Produces about 100 million litres a year, mostly strong, heady reds, which are dry to sweet. Quality is improving with gentler wood ageing.

Styles: *Reds*: Usually big, heady, tannic fruity wines but the better, lighter style is fruitier, less harsh with fuller flavour, and has ageing potential (C/E).

Whites: Resinated, full bodied, strong and dry to sweet. New blends and cool fermentation are producing crisper, lighter, fruitier styles. Drink young (2/8).

Mavrodaphne: Smooth, sweet, rich and heady. Drink youngish (8).

Muscat: Can be dry to sweet, but the best are heady, luscious and honeyed. Drink young (8).

11,4% vol.　　Product of Hungary　　75 cl

Tihanyi
CABERNET
dry quality red wine
Bottled by State Farm Badacsony

Hungary

History: Although vines have been grown for wine
in Hungary since Celtic times – before the Roman
invasion – it was the Magyars in the 9th century who
increased the vineyard acreage and production.
Many of the vineyards can trace their history back
centuries, and some as far back as the 12th century.
The Tokaj-Hagyalja region not only produces
Hungary's most famous wine, but is home to some
of the oldest vineyards which were planted at the end
of the 9th century. Phylloxera hit Hungary in the
1880s and destroyed three quarters of the vineyards.
Those which survived were mostly planted in very
sandy soil, through which the phylloxera bug cannot
travel.

Current situation: Hungary is striving to regain a
reputation largely built on Bull's Blood and Tokay
but which has slipped of late. There are 13 wine
growing regions with about 400,000 acres of
vineyards producing almost 450 million litres of
wine a year. About half the production is exported,

mostly to Eastern Europe although the emphasis is now to sell more to the West, especially medium price range wines. Vineyard area has halved in the past 20 years as growers concentrated on quality rather than quantity production. There have been extensive plantings of Chardonnay, Riesling and Traminer together with Cabernet Sauvignon and Pinot Noir. Most promising are Cabernets from Vilnay in the north east, Traminer from Sopron and fine whites from Lake Balaton.

Grapes: *Local varieties*: Furmint, Hárslevelü, Kadarka, Leanyka, Szürkebarát and Ezerjo.

Classic varieties: Cabernet Sauvignon, Cabernet Franc, Gewürztraminer, Merlot, Pinot Gris, Pinot Noir, Sauvignon Blanc and Sylvaner.

Regions: *Eger*: Famous for strong red Bull's Blood, but the quality is now very variable.
The Great Plain: A huge, sandy area resistant to vine diseases, which produces mostly white wine for bulk export to Germany for blending. Promising Riesling and some good light Cabernet.

Hungarian

PINOT BLANC
Dry White Wine

11,5% vol.   75 cl

Produced and bottled by: PANNONVIN CORP., Pécs
EXPORT: MONIMPEX
SOLE IMPORTERS: SIEBRAND (UK) LTD. MANCHESTER

Soltvadkerti Olaszrizling
Fehér félédes minőségi bor

Termelte és palackozta: SZÖLŐSKERT MEZŐGAZDASÁGI SZAKSZÖVETKEZET
SOLTVADKERT

ETK 88227 2636   GORDIUSZ--PETŐFI

Lake Balaton: The vineyards around Europe's largest
lake produce some of Hungary's best whites,
especially from Riesling, Furmint and Traminer.
Pecs: Produces some of the best Kadarka and
Cabernet Sauvignon.
Sopron: Hungary's oldest wine region, noted for
light, Beaujolais-style reds made from the
Kékfrancos grape, and rich, honeyed whites from
Traminer.
Tokay: In the north-east. A producer of one of the
world's great wines, which keeps on improving with
age but still retains freshness and fruit. The grapes
are picked late after being attacked by 'noble rot',
which concentrates the natural sugar. The grapes are
then left in small tubs (*putton*) where their own
weight extracts an intensely sweet juice. This essence
is drawn off and the grapes left are mashed and put
in a *gönc*, a 140 litre cask of dry base wine. Sweetness
is determined by the number of *putton*-loads of
essence which are added (*puttonyos*). The sweeter
the wine, the longer it needs to be aged.

Styles: *Cabernet Franc*: soft, light and pleasantly fruity. Drink youngish (C).

Cabernet Sauvignon: Complex rich fruit, blackcurranty with a hint of sweetness. Will age (D).

Merlot: Soft, fruity and easy drinking. Drink young (B).

Pinot Noir: Light-bodied, fruity and slightly, aromatic. Drink young (B).

Shiraz: Soft, full and fruity. Age well (D).

Kadarka: The most planted variety. Big, full flavoured, fruity, will age (D).

Chardonnay: Wood-matured and lively with good fruitoak balance. Drink youngish (2).

Furmint: Light, pungent and fresh with a hint of dry apricots. Age well (2).

Muscat: Fresh, flowery and medium sweet to sweet. Drink youngish (5/8).

Olasz Riesling: light, medium dry to sweet. Drink youngish (4/6).

Tokay: From dry to sweet, measured in Puttonyos up to 8 for Essencia. The sweetest has a sherry-like nose and is clean, luscious soft with rich fruit and a big, lingering finish. Age well (3/8).

Royal Maharashtra Mousseux
Sparkling Wine

OMAR KHAYYAM

Méthode Champenoise
Brut

750 ml   PRODUCE OF INDIA   12.5% vol
C.L LIMITED BOMBAY MAHARASHTRA INDIA

Sole Importer—Berkeley Wines Ltd., Croydon, Surrey, U.K.

India

History: A wine tradition dates back at least 2,000 years and the first vines were probably imported by the Greeks. Many of the early vineyards were planted in the far north, on the southern slopes of the Himalayas and Kashmir was still a wine producing region in the 19th century. The Moguls owned huge vineyard estates and in 1628 Emperor Jahangir was depicted on a coin holding a goblet of wine. Disease wiped out imported varieties in the late 19th century and the vineyard acreage steadily declined throughout the first half of the present century.

Current situation: Not normally thought of as a wine making country, India now has about 30,000 acres of vineyards, and the area is increasing, with local varieties being overtaken by classic European vines. It is only in the past ten years that the wines have been taken seriously abroad, largely because of a couple of Indo-French ventures. French grapes were planted on a carefully selected site in Maharashtra, where a multi-million pound modern winery was built, and India's first classy bottle fermented sparkling wine was created from Chardonnay and Ugni Blanc. It is dry, crisp and full of flavour and benefits from a little ageing. The vines are young and the wine is set to get even better (2).

Grapes: Cabernet Sauvignon, Chardonnay, Pinot Noir and Ugni Blanc.

Regions: The main vineyards are found around Madras, Maharashtra and Mysore. There are smaller plantings south of Bombay and near Delhi.

OMAR KHAYYAM

Royal Maharashtra Mousseux
Sparkling Wine

The vineyards on the upper slopes of the Sahyadri Mountains in Western Maharashtra have been famous for centuries, supplying wine to the courts of the Grand Moghuls including that of Shah Jehan, the builder of the Taj Mahal

Nowadays however, the principal grapes used are of pure Chardonnay stock, specially imported from France and the most modern Methode Champenoise technology is used to ensure a consistently high quality product

The special reserve of this wine, kept solely for export, is dedicated to the famous Persian poet and scientist Omar Khayyam whose verses in praise of such wines are immortalized in his celebrated Rubaiyat

Drink wine that is life everlasting
The source of youthful delight

Sole Importers: BERKELEY WINES LIMITED.
Lynton House, 304 Bensham Lane, Thornton Heath, Surrey, CR4 7YR. Tel: 01-683 0494

Ben Ami בן עמי

SAMSON REGION

11.3% VOL.750ML e כשר לפסח

PRODUCED & BOTTLED BY ASKALON WINES CARMEI ZION LTD RAMLE ISRAEL

Israel

History: It is not known when the first vines were
cultivated in Israel but the wine-making tradition
could date back to almost 3,000 BC. Biblical records
of vineyards and wine are plentiful. In 1800 BC there
are accounts of vineyards in Palestine where there
was more wine than water, and in 1500 BC it was
recorded that the Gardens of Canaan had cellars
where the wine flowed liked waterfalls. Palestinian
wines were exported throughout the Middle East,
and even to England up to about AD 600, when the
country was conquered by Arabs and Moslem law
decreed that all the vineyards be destroyed. There
were a few vineyards around Bethlehem during the
Crusades in the 13th century, but it was not until the
1880s when Baron Edmond de Rothschild built
wineries on Mount Carmel that wine-making took
off again.

Current situation: Traditionally known for mostly
sweet wines, Israel has made great strides in recent

years towards drier, fruitier styles especially using classic varieties of grapes. It is one of the wonders of the world that Israel manages to produce grapes at all in places like the rainless, sun baked Negev Desert. Today the vineyards are being planted at altitude, on the Golan Heights for instance, away from the hot coastal belt, and the results have been very good. Full fruited Golan Cabernet Sauvignon, aged in new oak, is the star performer (C) followed by crisp, fruity Sauvignon Blanc (1). Israel produces all styles of wine. There are acceptable wines from around Haifa and Galilee which is producing good Cabernets. Exports are dominated by Carmel which operates throughout Britain, the United States and Canada. Overall exports are increasing.

Grapes: *Classic varieties*: Alicante, Cabernet Sauvignon, Carignan

Regions: Allah, Beersheba, Galilee, Golan Heights, Jerusalem, Negev, Richon-le-Zion, Sydoon-Gezer, Zefat, Zichron-Jacob.

DISTILLED & BOTTLED BY ASKALON WINES-CARMEL ZION LTD, ISRAEL

hallelujah

LIQUEUR

70 U.S. PROOF 35% ALC. BY VOL. 750 ml.

RISERVA

Vigneti

La Selvanella

V LOCALITÀ SELVANELLA V

Chianti classico

DENOMINAZIONE DI ORIGINE CONTROLLATA
E GARANTITA

Questa bottiglia porta il numero D 11782

IMBOTTIGLIATO NELLE PROPRIE CANTINE DI GAGGIANO - ITALIA DA

Melini s.c.a.r.l.

ITALIA

0.750 ℓ · e   12.5% vol

Italy

History: The Greeks introduced vines to Italy about 3,000 years ago and called the country '*Enotria Tellus*', the land of vines. The vineyards were concentrated in the south, and it was the Etruscans who planted vines in the central and northern regions. Wine making has enjoyed an unbroken tradition ever since.

Current situation: The world's largest wine producer although rapidly being overtaken by the Soviet Union. There are six main regions, divided into 20 major wine areas. More than 1.2 million vineyards cover 2.5 million acres – the world's third largest wine-growing area – although only 15 per cent of producers – about 11,000 – bottle their own wine. Production peaked in 1980 at 8,650 million litres but recent harvests have yielded about 6,000 million litres of wine. During the 1980s up to a quarter of the production went for distillation and most of the wine exported was shipped out in bulk for blending, mainly in France and Germany. Wine consumption in Italy has fallen sharply in the past decade, as have exports, and efforts are now concentrated on reducing quantity and raising quality. Having said that, however, Italy boasts many world class wines, many deservedly recognised and others seriously underrated. Italy produces wines of every style and taste from light, delicate whites to big, full-bodied, long lasting reds. Also popular is the wide range of sparkling wine, especially the increasingly popular *spumante*.

Classification: Quality wine laws were introduced in 1963, but quickly lost credibility, and Italy is now having to work hard worldwide to re-establish its reputation. Many of its finest wines do not qualify for quality status either because of the grape variety used or the wine-making techniques. The quality laws are based heavily on traditional vine-growing and wine-making techniques rather than on the quality of the product in the bottle. Little control was exercised over which wines received quality status, and no attempt was made to reduce vineyard yields and raise quality.

A higher quality category was introduced in the late 1970s and has improved the situation, although why some wines have won this higher classification and others not is a mystery.

There are now about 250 quality wines or wine producing areas classified, and a further six with the higher quality rating, which together account for just over 10 per cent of Italy's total production. The Government aims to increase quality output to at least 20 per cent of all production, and wants to see a further 40 per cent of wine qualify for basic *vin da tavola* status.

(Vdt) Vini da tavola: Covering all table wines and much bulk wine for blending. If the label bears no other information treat with caution, but Sassicaia, made from Cabernet Sauvignon, is also sold under this classification and I think this Tuscan offering is one of the great wines of Italy.

Vini da tavola con indicazione Geografica: From a particular area. The label may specify grape variety.

Vini tipici: A new category supposedly equivalent to the French *Vin de Pays*, although open to much wider interpretation.

(DOC) Denominazione di Origine Controllata: Wines from specified areas and made from an agreed list of grape varieties. Grape yields are controlled but are too high, and producers are allowed to exceed

them by up to 20 per cent in 'exceptional' years. A single DOC area can include wines of totally different style and quality but all are allowed the classification.

(DOCG) Denominazione di Origine Controllata e Garantita: A category with teeth and much stricter regulations. So far, five reds have qualified for DOCG status – Barolo, Barbaresco, Brunello di Montalconi, Chianti and Vino Nobile di Montepulciano – and one white, Albana di Romagna. Many others are in the wings. Producers have to submit their wines to a tasting panel before being awarded the quality seal and not all are approved.

Understanding the label

abboccato	–	medium sweet
amabile	–	between abbocato and dolce
annata	–	year of vintage
azienda	–	the estate or vineyard
bianco	–	white
cantina	–	winery
casa vinicola	–	a house that buys in grapes or wine
cerasuolo	–	rosé (also chiaretto)
classico	–	the traditional area of production
consorzio	–	a group of growers that oversee production regulations
dolce	–	sweet
frizzante	–	semi-sparkling, usually from second fermentation in the tank
imbottigliato	–	bottled
invecchiato	–	aged
liquorose	–	a high strength wine, often fortified
metodo classico	–	méthode champenoise sparkling wine
riserva	–	a reserve wine often aged longer than normal
rosato	–	rosé
secco	–	dry
spumante	–	sparkling
superiore	–	usually a DOC wine
vecchio	–	old
vendemmia	–	the vintage

Grapes: There are about 1,000 different grape varieties grown throughout the country, of which about 400 are approved for one or more of the regions. The principal varieties of each region are dealt with below.

NORTH WEST ITALY
This area covers Piedmont, Liguria, Lombardy and
the Valle d'Aosta. There are about 260,000 acres of
vineyards and annual production tops 650 million
litres.

Piedmont: **Grapes**: *Barbera: Soft, fruity and*
youthful. Can be fine, big, robust and long living.
Moscato: Light, aromatic, grapey, sweet spumante.
The backbone of Asti.
Nebbiolo: Italy's noblest red with a big rich flavour,
producing tarry Barolo and elegant, fruity
Barbaresco.
Cabernet Sauvignon, *Cabernet Franc* and *Merlot* are
increasingly used by top producers to add elegance,
and experiments with wood ageing are producing
very good whites made from Chardonnay and Pinot
Bianco.

Styles: *Arneis*: Soft and delicate with big ripe fruit.
Flavourful. Drink youngish (2).
Asti Spumante: Frothy, fruity, grapey, sweet and
fun. Drink young (7).

CASTELGREVE

RISERVA 1985

CHIANTI CLASSICO

DENOMINAZIONE DI ORIGINE CONTROLLATA E GARANTITA

D.O.C.G.

750 ml ℮   IMBOTTIGLIATO DAI PRODUTTORI RIUNITI CASTELLI DEL GREVEPESA   12,5% vol.
S.C.R.L. - MERCATALE VAL DI PESA - R.I. 28/FI - ITALIA

Barbaresco: Harshness can mask smoky fruitiness when young. Must be aged at least two years, one of them in wood. With age it can become elegant, soft and fruity (C).

Barbera: Big and raspy when young; big and rich, rounded and fruity with age (D).

Barolo: Big, powerful and full of fruit with great longevity (E).

Carema: Soft, light and fruity with a big bouquet. Best after about 5 years (C).

Cortese di Gavi: Soft and dry, with a slight fizz; rich and honeyed after a little bottle age, drink youngish (3).

Dolcetto: Soft, very fresh and fruity, drink young (B).

Erbaluce di Caluso: Light, fresh and dry with creamy fruit. Also some sweet, drink young (2/7).

Gattinara: Earthy and fruity when young; fine and silky-perfumed when aged (C).

Moscato d'Asti: Les fizz than Asti Spumante. Fresh, rich and spicy. Drink young (7).

Spanna: Good value. Big, tasty Barola-like wine. Drink youngish (C/E).

Liguria: The strip of mountainous land running round the coast from Tuscany to the French border with Genoa at its heart. Main red varieties are Rossese, Ormeasco and Sangiovese, and for whites, Bosco, Pigato, Trebbiano Toscano and Vermentino.

Styles: *Cinqueterre*: Mostly from the Bosco grape. Delicate, fragrant, dry or medium. Drink young (3/6).
Colli di Luni: Dry, crisp wines, red, white and rosé. Drink young (3/B).
Riviera Ligure di Ponente: Dry, fruity reds which age well; whites which are big, rich and dry. Drink young (3/B).
Rossesse di Dolceacqua: Big bouquet, rich wines. Soft fruity and spicy. Drink youngish (B).

Lombardy: More than 75,000 acres of vineyards sprawling around Milan on the plains of the Po Valley. There are three sub-regions: Oltrepò Pavese in the south-west for red, white and spumante, Valtellina in the Alps to the north for good reds; and Brescia to the east with seven of Lombardy's 13 DOCs.
The main grapes are Nebbiola, Barbera, Cabernet Franc, Merlot and Cabernet Sauvignon for red and rosé, and Pinot Bianco, Chardonnay, Riesling Italico and Pinot Grigio for white and sparkling wines.

Styles: *Botticino*: Big, full-bodied and strong. Age well (C).
Capriano del Colle: Light, dry, fruity lively reds. Drink young (B).
Cellatica: Light, delicate and fruity. Drink young (B).
Colli Morenici Mantovani del Garda: simple dry red, white and rosé (3/C).
Franciacorta: Big and rich with curranty fruit. Age well with finesse (C).
Lambrusco Mantovano: Light, fruity dry to sweet. Drink young (A).
Lugana: Well made, dry, crisp, flavourful and fruity. Drink young (3).

CASTELLO
DI QUERCETO
Chianti Classico
denominazione di origine controllata e garantita
1986

ITALIA
750 ml ℮   12% vol.

Maurizio Zanella: Full and fruity. A very classy wine. Ages well (D).

Oltrepò Parvese: Dry red and rosé, dry to sweet white and fine, dry traditional method sparkling. Most should be drunk young, although sweet whites age.

Riviera del Garda Bresciano: Large, variable, generic GOC. Dry reds, delicate rosé. Drink young (C/3).

San Colombano: Sturdy, earthy reds. Drink youngish (C).

Valccalepio: Big, full flavoured reds (Merlot and Cabernet Sauvignon) which age well; and light, delicate whites (C/3).

Valtellina: Elegant, light and aromatic. Age well (B).

Tocai di San Martino della Battaglia: Dry, aromatic and flowery (3).

Valle d'Aosta: An area of 2,500 acres of vineyards trapped in the Alps. The Valle d'Aosta DOC covers 18 different wines. A number of imported classic varieties do well here, especially Gamay, Pinot Noir and Müller Thurgau, but the main varieties from the 22 which are approved are Blanc de Morgex, Fumin, Malvoisie, Moscato di Chambave and Petit Rouge.

The reds tend to be dry, youthful and fruity; the whites crisp, aromatic and dry through to rich, long lived sweet wines.

Styles: *Blanc de Morgex*: Dry, crisp, fruity, slightly frizzante. Drink young (2).
Chambave: Aromatic, crisp, rich and fruity. Will age (C).
Malvoise de Nus: Luscious, rich, dessert wine with great longevity (8).
Torrette: Dry, rounded, fruity and full bodied. Drink young (B).

NORTH EAST ITALY

A mainly mountainous region stretching from the Dolomites and the Austrian border south to Venice and Trieste. The high vineyards are noted for their crisp, full flavoured whites, although most production comes from the Veneto in the shape of Soave and Valpolicella, the majority of which is exported. There are three main sub-regions; Trentino-Alto Adige, the Veneto and Friuli-Venezia Giulia. There are about 310,000 acres of vineyards, and annual production tops 1,100 million litres, of

AZIENDA AGRICOLA
dei Conti
GUERRIERI-RIZZARDI

Valpolicella
Denominazione di Origine Controllata
V. Q. P. R. D.
Classico Superiore

0,750 lt.

Imbottigliato all'origine dal viticoltore
Guerrieri Rizzardi - Bardolino
ITALIA

12 % vol.

VINO NON PASTORIZZATO

which the 32 DOCs account for about a quarter. It is an exciting region with a lot of experimentation with classic French and German grape varieties and showing great promise.

Trentino-Alto Adige: A mountainous area of about 35,000 acres of vineyards, which used to be the Austrian province of South Tyrol and is still German-speaking. To avoid any confusion, the wine makers are now promoting the name Alto Adige. Italian-speaking Trentino is its southern neighbour. Alto Adige wines are made from single grape varieties.

Grapes: *Red*: *Cabernet Sauvignon*: Rich, deep, full bodied and fruity. Age well.
Cabernet Franc: Soft, fruity and spicy. Mellow and full bodied with age.
Lagrein Dunkel: Big and fruity. Will age.
Malvasia: Dry to very sweet wines. Big, fruity, sweet wines age well.
Merlot: Soft, light and fruity. Age well.
Pinot Nero: Light, fruity and scented. Age well.

Schiava (Vernatsch): Light, juicy and fruity. Drink youngish.
Rose: Lagrein Rosato: Smooth, fruity and medium-bodied. Drink young.
Pinot Nero: Light, elegant, perfumed and fruity.
Moscato Rosa: Very aromatic and fruity. Medium sweet to sweet. Drink young.
White: Chardonnay: Light, crisp and fruity, from dry to spumante. Drink young.
Moscato Giallo: Makes luscious, sweet, dessert wines with great longevity.
Pinot Bianco: Fine, crisp, fragrant, fruity and classy. Drink youngish.
Pinot Grigio: Soft and full fruited with low acid. Drink young.
Riesling Renano: Italy's best Riesling. Elegant, fresh, crisp and fruity. Will age in good years.
Müller Thurgau: Declining acreage. Spicy, aromatic and fruity. Drink young.
Sauvignon blanc: Classy, crisp, fresh and fruity. Drink young.
Silvaner: Fresh, lively and fruity. Drink young.
Traminer (Gewürztraminer): Light, delicate, aromatic and spicy with subtle fruit. Drink young, but it will age.

Styles: *Alto Adige (Südtiroler)*: Dry, crisp, aromatic whites; soft, light, fruity reds; and flowery, aromatic, fruity rosé (3/B).
Caldaro (Kalteress): Soft, easy drinking and fruity. Drink young (B).
Casteller: Light and fruity red and rosé. Drink young (B).
Colli di Bolzano: Soft, light and fruity. Drink very young (A).
Meranese di Collina: Light, perfumed and fruity. Drink young (B).
Santa Maddalena: Smooth, big-bodied and full-flavoured. Will age (D).
Sorni: Soft, light fruity reds and delicate, fresh whites. Drink young (B/3).
Teroldego Rotaliano: Big, full-bodied and fruity. Will age (C).

CHIANTI
CLASSICO
DENOMINAZIONE DI ORIGINE CONTROLLATA E GARANTITA
CERASI
1986
IMBOTTIGLIATO DALLA
FATTORIA CONCADORO S.R.L.
CASTELLINA IN CHIANTI - ITALIA
0,750 Litri ℮   R.I.370.SI   12% VOL.

Terlano: Good, soft, varietal reds; and dry, fruity, blended whites. Drink young (B/3).
Trentino: Light, fruity reds; and crisp, dry whites. Drink young. Many other styles produced (B/3).
Valdadige: Soft, light and fruity reds; and crisp, dry to semi-sweet whites. Drink young (B/3).
Valle Isarco: Good varietal dry whites and reds. Drink young (3/B).

The Veneto: A huge wine producing region on the plains behind Venice with 225,000 acres of vineyards yielding more than 900 million litres of wine. It is Italy's largest producer of DOC wines, thanks to Soave, Valpolicella and Bardolino. Merlot and Cabernet Sauvignon produce light, fruity everyday drinking reds and fresh, crisp Chardonnay. Native grapes such as Corvina and Rondinella predominate in Bardolino and Valpolicella, and Garganega in Soave. Prosecco produces many of the best soft sparkling wines.

Styles: *Bardolino*: Medium-bodied, fresh and fruity when young. Age well (A).

Bianco di Custoza: Perfumed, fruity, dry and sparkling (2).

Breganze: Blended and varietal dry red and white. Drink young (C/3).

Colli Berici: Red and white varietals plus a rich, fruity Cabernet. Drink young (C).

Colli Euganei: Soft, full-bodied dry to medium sweet blended red and white. A number of red and white varietals (A/C; 2/7).

Gambellara: Perfumed, crisp dry to raisin sweet and spumante (3/8).

Lessini Durello: Sharp, refreshing dry (2).

Montello e Colli Asolani: Good red and white varietals. Reds age well (C/3).

Piave: Good Raboso, Merlot and Cabernet varietals. Drink young (C).

Prosecco di Conegliano: Big, earthy, bubbly sparklers. Dry to medium (2/6).

Soave: Light, fresh and subtle fruit. Classico is bigger, and new oak can do wonders (2).

Tocai di San Martino della Battaglia: Light and dry with slight bitterness (2).

Valdadige: Light, dry everyday drinking red and white. Dry to medium (C/3).

Valpolicella: Enormously variable. Should be light, delicate and nutty. Classico is better and superiore is stronger and older. Drink young (B).

Friuli-Venezia Giulia: Just over 53,000 acres of vineyards north of Trieste. Almost half its production is for DOC wines and it produces many good classic varietals.

Styles: *Aquiileia*: Well made, light, balanced red, white and rosé varietals. Drink young (C/3).

Carso: Big, rich, fruity reds which age; and rich, honeyed white. Drink young (D/4).

Collio: Large range of blended varietal dry red and white. Drink young (C/3).

Colli Orientali del Friuli: Wide range of whites, blends and varietals. Good fresh, zesty Chardonnay. Drink young (2/3).

Grave del Friuli: Large range of varietal dry red and white. Good Merlot. Drink youngish (B).

Isonzo: Red and white varietals. Dry, good Merlot
and Cabernet. Drink youngish (B).
Latisana: good red and white varietals. Drink
youngish (3/B).
Lison-Pramaggiore: Big, rich reds,which age well;
and light, dry, fruity whites (3/C).

CENTRAL ITALY

The central part of Italy incorporates two wine
growing regions – the Adriatic Appenines down the
eastern half of the country, and the Central
Tyrrhenian in the west. The first covers the sub-
regions of Emilia-Romagna, the Marches, Abruzzi
and Molise, home of Lambrusco, while the second is
dominated by the sub-region of Tuscany, famous for
Chianti, plus Ubrium and Latium.

Emilia-Romagna: About 190,000 acres of
vineyards surrounding Bologna producing about 850
million litres of wine a year. The three main grape
varieties are Albana, Lambrusco and Trebbiano
producing dry, generally unexciting whites.
Saniovese, especially when blended with Cabernet,
produces very classy reds which have enormous
potential.

Styles: *Albana di Romagna*: Dry, fruity and
undeserving of DOCG status. Drink young (2).
Bianco di Scandiano: Big and fruity. Dry to
medium; can be spumante. Drink young (3).
Bosco Eliceo: Big, strong, full bodied and fruity.
Will age (D).
Cagnina di Romagna: Soft, warm, fresh and fruity
with a touch of violets and sweetness. Drink young
(C).
Colli Bolognesi: A number of red and white
varietals. Drink young (C/3).
Colli di Parma: Fine, slightly fizzy whites from
Malvasia and Sauvignon. Drink young (2).
Colli Piacentini: A wide range of varietals and
blends, mostly dry. Drink young (C/3).
Lambrusco: Hugely popular in UK and US. Frothy,
cherry fruit. Sweet (A).

Lambrusco Grasparossa di Castelvetro: Slightly less fizz; dry to medium (A)

Lambrusco Reggiano: The lightest of Lambruscos. Red or rosé; dry to medium (A).

Lambrusco Salamino di Santa Croce: Classy, aromatic Lambrusco (A).

Lambrusco di Sorbara: The best Lambrusco. Dry to medium (A).

Montuni del Reno: Frizzante, fruity and dry to sweet. Drink young (3/7).

Ronco Armantano: Soft, aromatic, fruity Sangiovese/Cabernet Franc cross. Age well (C).

Sangiovese di Romagne: Big, full fruity reds. Age well (D).

Terre Rosse Chardonnay: Good Chardonnay. Dry and full-flavoured. Drink youngish (2).

Trebbiano di Romagna: Light and fruity, dry to sweet and spumante. Drink young (27).

The Marches: An area which has long produced good drinking wines such as Verdicchio for the tourists and locals. The main red varieties are Sangiovese and Montepulciano; and the main whites are Trebbiano Toscano and Verdicchio.

Styles: *Bianchello del Metauro*: Light, dry and slightly lemony. Drink young (3).

Bianco dei Colli Maceratsei: Dry, white and refreshing. Drink young (3).

Faleiro dei Colli Ascolani: Dry, aromatic and fruity. Drink young (3).

Lacrima di Morro d'Alba: Soft, warm and fruity. Drink young (B).

Rosso Cònero: Classy reds: big, rich and full-bodied. Age well (D).

Rosso Piceno: Big and round with full fruit. Age well (C).

Sangiovese dei Colli Pesaresi: Classy and fruity. Needs a litte time to soften (C).

Verdicchio dei Castelli di Jesi: Produces a wide range of styles. Popular locally. Light, crisp, fruity Verdicchio is the best (3).

Verdicchio di Matelica: Classy whites which are fruity with good acidity. Will age (2).

NEGRO

ROERO ARNEIS
Denominazione d'Origine Controllata
1989

Imbottigliato all'origine
dall'Azienda Agricola Negro Angelo e Figli
Fraz. S. Anna - Monteu Roero (CN) - Italia

750 ml ℮   12% vol.

NON DISPERDERE IL VETRO

Vernaccia di Serrapetrona: Aromatic and fruity. Dry to spumante (A/B).

Abruzzi: An area of hilly vineyards with Montepulciano the main variety, followed by Trebbiano.

Styles: *Montepulciano d'Abruzzo*: Big, soft, velvety, fruity reds that age well; and fresh, delicate, dry rosé which should be drunk young (B).
Trebbiano d'Abruzzo: Dry, light on fruit. Drink young (2).

Molise: A rustic, hilly area with 25,000 acres of vines. Most production is drunk locally or sent to Abruzzi for blending.

Styles: *Biferno*: Smooth, light reds; and dry, fruity white and rosé. Drink young (C/3).
Pentro di Isernia: Dry, fruity red and rosé, high in tannin; and crisp fresh white. All should be drunk young (C/3).

Tuscany: A major wine region producing almost 400 million litres a year, of which just under a quarter is for DOC and DOCG wines. Tuscany has three of Italy's six DOCGs. Traditionally famous for Chianti, Tuscany has many experimental vineyards and produces many spectacular wines, including the magnificent Sassicaia made from Cabernet Sauvignon which is classy, complex and improves with age. The region's main grapes are Malvasia, Sangiovese and Trebbiano.

Styles: *Bianco della Valdinievole*: Light, dry and lacking depth. Drink young (2).
Bianco dell'Empolese: Light, dry and lacklustre. Drink young (2).
Bianco Pisano di San Torpè: Light with subtle fruit. Dry to medium (3/5).
Bianco Vergine Valdichiana: Dry, white, fruity and sometimes frizzante. Drink young (2).
Bolgheri: Fine, dry and aromatic. Drink young (3).
Brunello di Montalcino: Big, rich, fruity and smokey. Need time to mature (E).
Candia dei Colli Apuani: Light and aromatic. Dry to medium. Drink young (3/5).
Carmignano: Classy, fruity and balanced. Age well (D).
Chianti: Very variable. At best medium-bodied and rich with plummy fruit. Drink youngish. Classico has more depth, complexity and staying power. Age well (D).
Colline Lucchesi: Light, fruity, Chianti style. Drink young (D).
Elba: Chianti style fruity reds. Drink young. Dry, light white. Drink young. Fruity, bubbly sparkling red. Drink young (D/3).
Montecarlo: Dry, aromatic, light whites. Drink young. Classy reds with hint of Burgundy. Will age (3/B).
Montescudaio: Dry, clingy whites. Soft, fruity reds. Drink young (2/B).
Morellino de Scansano: Full-bodied and richly fruity. Age well (E).
Moscadello di Montalcino: Perfumed, sweet and still to sparkling. Drink young (7).

Parrina: Soft, fruity, delicate reds; and dry, crisp whites. Drink young (B/2).

Pomino: Classy, fruity blended red and white; dry to medium (A/C; 2/6).

Rosso di Montalcino: Big and fruity, long lasting reds (D).

Rosso di Montepulciano: Big and rich with plummy fruit. Long lasting (D).

Vernaccia di San Gimignano: Dry, crisp and fruity, Drink young (2).

Vino Nobile di Montpulciano: Like the best Chianti Classico. Long-lasting (D).

Umbria: An area of 55,000 acres of vine surrounding Perugia. Just over 10 per cent of production is for DOC wines. Orvieto is the most famous wine, although overrated, and there is a lot of promising experimentation going on especially using new oak barrels.

Styles: *Colli Altotiberini*: Dry, crisp whites. Dry, soft, fruity red and rosé. Drink young (2/B).

Colli del Trasimeno: Dry, fresh white; and soft, big-fruit reds. Drink young (2/A).

Colli Martani: Promising dry white and red. Drink young (3/B).

Colli Perugini: Dry, fruity white; big, rich red; and dry delicate rosé. Drink young (3/C).

Montefalco: Dry, rich, full-fruited red made from Sagrantino. Will age (C).

Orvieto: Smooth and fruity with some depth. Dry to medium (3/5).

Torgiano: Classy red and dry white. Drink young (C/3).

Latium: The large wine-producing area surrounding Rome. Home of Frascati and some interesting French blends, especially Cabernet Sauvignon and Merlot.

Styles: *Aleatico di Gradoli*: Soft, fruity, aromatic and sweet. Age well (D).

Aprilia: Red and white varietals which lack fruit. Drink young (B/3).

Bianco Capena: Light, fruity, dry to medium. Drink young (3/5).

Cerveteri: Earthy, fruity red; and dry, fruity whites. Drink young (C/3).

Cesanese del Piglio: Light, fruity, dry to sweet and spumante. Drink young (A/B).

Cesanese di Affile: As above (A/B).

Colli Albani: Soft, fruity and dry. Drink young (3).

Colli Lanuvini: Smooth and fruity; dry to medium. Drink young (3/6).

Est! Est!! Est!!!: Soft, fruity; dry to medium. Drink young (3/6).

Frascati: Very variable. Should be soft, richly fruity; dry to sweet. Drink youngish (2/7).

Marino: Upmarket Frascati. Dry to medium or spumante. Drink young (3/5).

Montecompatri Colonna: Soft, fruity, rich, dry and medium, spumante. Drink young (2/7).

Orvieto: Big, rich, fruity; dry to medium. Drink young (3/5).

Velletri: Dry, fruity red and smooth dry to medium white. Drink young (B; 3/5).

Zagarolo: Frascati-style (2/7).

MOSCATO D'ASTI

Denominazione d'origine controllata
imbottigliato dal produttore Azienda Agricola GATTI PIERO

Vigneto Moncucco   **1988**   S. Stefano Belbo (CN) - Italia

L'etichetta è stata realizzata dal pittore venezuelano Simon Hernandez

75 CL. ℮   5,5 % Volume

SOUTHERN ITALY

This area includes the south of Italy and the sub-regions of Apulia, Campania, Basilcata and Calabria, together with the islands of Sardinia and Sicily. It covers more than 1.1 million acres of wine and produces almost 3,000 litres of wine. Long hot, dry summers produce big, powerful, full-flavoured wines but massive yields often affect quality. Careful attention in the vineyard, irrigation and better wine making techniques have led to a growing number of good wines with promise.

Apulia: Italy's largest wine producing region, with Bari as its capital. In 1986 it produced a record 1,400 million litres of wine. DOC wines represent less than 2 per cent of production, but a vast range of grape varieties (including classic varieties from France and imports from California and Germany) means there is enormous scope for experimentation. The main varieties are Primitivo (the Californian Zinfandel) and Uva di Troia.

Styles: *Aleatico di Puglia*: Big, rich and aromatic; medium to sweet. Drink young (B).
Alezio: Dry, fruity red and delicate rosé. Drink young (B).
Brindisi: Soft, fruity red; and dry, light, fruity rosé. Drink young (B).
Cacc'e Mmitte di Lucera: Soft, fruity and blended. Drink young (B).
Castel del Monte: Big, robust reds which will age; and dry fruity white and rosé. Drink young (D/3).
Copertino: Big, rich, dry red; and delicate rosé. Drink young (C).
Leverano: Big, rich, fruity reds. Drink youngish. Dry, fruity white and rosé. Drink young (D/3).
Lizzano: Covers a number of dry red, white and rosé. Drink young (D/3).
Martina Franca: Light and dry, with subdued fruit. Can be spumante (3).
Matino: Sturdy, fruity red and rosé. Drink youngish (C).
Moscato di Trani: Big, perfumed, dessert wine. Sweet (7).

Nardò: Big and strong. Will age (D).

Orta Nova: Big, fruity, dry red and rosé. Drink youngish (C).

Ostuni: Dry, delicate whites; and dry, cherry fruit reds. Drink young (2/B).

Primitivo di Manduria: Big, fruity reds. Dry to medium. Drink youngish (C).

Rosso Barletta: Quaffing wines. Dry with juicy fruity. Drink very young (B).

Rosso Canosa: Dry, rich and fruity. Age well (C).

Rosso di Cergnola: Big, strong and sturdy. Drink youngish (C).

Salice Salentino: Big, strong red and rosé. Aged Reserva smoother (D).

San Severo: Light, dry red, white and rosé. Drink young (B/3).

Squinzano: Big sturdy, fruity red which will age. Light, delicate rosé. Drink young (D).

Gioia del Colle: Covers many styles: dry white and rosé; and dry to sweet reds. Drink young (3; A/D).

Campania: A big producing region surrounding Naples, which imports more wine than it produces. Much of 'home' production is uninspiring.

Styles: *Aglianico del Taburno*: Dry, light red and rosé. Drink young (B).

Capri: Light, fruity, good quaffing red and white. Drink young (B/3).

Cilento: Fruity spumante red and rosé. Dry to medium. Drink young (B).

Falerno del Massico: Big, rich, sturdy reds which will age. Light, dry white. Drink young (D/3).

Fiano di Avellino: Best white in the south. Aromatic, nutty, spicy with a hint of pears. Mellows with ageing (3).

Greco di Tufo: Crisp and full fruit with a hint of toasted almonds. Drink youngish (3).

Ischia: Fairly full, fruity reds. Dry, light-fruited white. Drink young (C/2).

Solopaca: Soft, fruity dry red and white. Drink young (C/3).

Taurasi: Big and classy, with intense bouquet and flavours. Great longevity (D).

Vesuvio: Wide range of wines from the slopes of the volcano.

Basilcata: A mountainous region of vineyards surrounding Potenza. There are more than 40,000 acres of vineyards but it is a very poor region and neither vineyards nor wineries have had the investment they require.

The only DOC: Agelianico del Vulture: Big and rich with cherry fruit. Develops powerful bouquet with ageing in wood. Five-year-old Reserva is very classy. Age well (D).

Calabria: More than 75,000 acres of vineyards around Catanzaro. Much of the production is uninspiring. The main grape is Gaglioppo, an ancient variety.

Styles: Cirò: Big, strong dry red, white and rosé. Will age (D/3).

Donnici: Dry, fruity red and rosé. Drink young (C).

Greco di Bianco: Sweet with a big bouquet of herbs and citrus. Drink youngish (7).

Lamezia: Soft, light, delicate red (A).

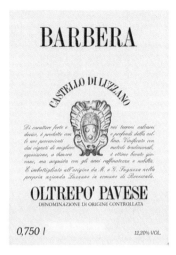

Melissa: Big, sturdy red which will age. Fresh, crisp, dry white. Drink young (D/2).

Pollino: Strong, sturdy and fruity. Can age but often oxidises (D).

Sant'Anna di Isola Capo Rizzuto: Light, dry red and rosé. Drink young (B).

Savuto: Light to medium red and rosé. Good fruit and body. Drink youngish (B).

Sardinia: A lot of investment in wineries has transformed the island's wines. Cool fermentation and stainless steel tanks has produced many fresh and fruity wines with good fruit and flavour.

Styles: *Arborea*: New DOC. Light, dry, fruity red, white and rosé. Drink young (B/3).

Campidano di Terralba: Smooth, big and fruity. Will age (D).

Cannonau di Sardegna: White, red and rosé from dry to sweet. Drink young.

Carignano del Sulcis: Light, dry, grapey red and rosé. Drink youngish (B).

Girò di Cagliari: Light, easy-drinking red and rosé. Dry to sweet. Will age (B).

GRAVE DEL FRIULI
DENOMINAZIONE DI ORIGINE CONTROLLATA
PINOT BIANCO

TRATTO DAI PROPRI
VIGNETI DI ONTAGNANO
PER LA RISERVA *di Lenardo*

1989   12.5 % vol.

Mandrolisai: Dry, light, fruity red and rosé. Will age (B).

Monica di Sardegna: Dry, soft, light and fruity. Drink youngish (B).

Malvasia di Bosa: Dry to sweet and fortified. Rich and full-flavoured. Will age (2/8).

Malvasia di Cagliari: Big, strong whites; dry to sweet. Drink youngish (3/7).

Moscato di Cagliari: Big, rich, dessert wine. Age well (8).

Moscato di Sardegna: Aromatic, sweet, fruity spumante. Drink young (7).

Moscato di Sorso-Sennori: Sweet and honeyed. Will age (7).

Monica di Cagliari: Soft, delicate and perfumed. Dry to sweet. Drink young (3/7).

Nasco di Cagliari: Delicate, subtly perfumed white; dry to sweet. Drink young (3/7).

Nuragus di Cagliari: Fresh, with a hint of lemon, Dry to medium, Drink young (3/5).

Vermentino di Gallura: Dry, light whites. Drink young (3).

Vermentino di Sardegna: Lightweight, dry to sweet. Drink young (3/7).

Vernaccia di Oristano: Sherry-like; dry to sweet, nutty and spicy. Will age (2/8).

Sicily: A massive wine producer, with much drunk on the island by locals and tourists.

Styles: *Alcamo*: Dry and fruity. Drink young (3).
Cerasuolo di Vittoria: Cherry red with some depth. Drink young (C).
Etna: Dry, full, fruity red and rosé; and soft, dry white. Drink young (C/3).
Faro: Fragrant and medium-bodied. Will age (B).
Malvasia delle Lipari: Strong, sweet and perfumed. Will age (7).
Marsala: Sherry-style, from dry to sweet, young to aged, red and white. Good aperitif or dessert wine (2/8).
Moscato di Noto: Perfumed and fragrant; still and spumante. Drink young (7).
Moscato di Pantelleria: Classy Moscato. Perfumed and medium to sweet. Drink young (5/7).
Moscato di Siracusa: Delicate and sweet. Drink young (7).

Best Recent Vintages: (for reds) 1988, 1985, 1983, 1981, 1978 (only 1984 and 1980 could be considered poor).

Japan

History: Vines have been cultivated since the 12th century but the grapes were mostly used for decoration or medicinal purposes. The local variety Koshu can be traced back to 1186. Wine making did not start in earnest until the 19th century when the first Europeans arrived. Japanese wine-makers were sent abroad to study in France and California and a vigorous vineyard-planting programme was launched with American hybrids and some European varieties.

Current situation: Japan has more than 75,000 acres of vineyards, and the acreage is increasing rapidly. Many of the vineyards, however, are small and poorly located. Annual production is about 20 million litres of wine. Japan produces some very good wines, mostly blends of locally produced wine and imported grape must, much of it from Chile and Australia. Hardly any is exported. Japanese wine laws allow a wine to be labelled 'Japanese' provided it contains 10 per cent of locally produced wine. There is an increasing trend, however, to produce 100 per cent Japanese wines and classic European varietals. Best results to date have come from Cabernet Sauvignon and Sémillon.

Grapes: Main European grapes are Cabernet Franc, Cabernet Sauvignon and Merlot for reds; and Chardonnay, Riesling, Sauvignon Blanc and Sémillon for whites. American hybrids include Campbells Early, Delaware, Muscat Bailey and Concord. Koshu is the most popular indigenous variety.

Regions: Hokkaido (Kushiro and Sapporo), Honshu (Kofu Valley, Nagano, Okayama, Osaka, Tokyo, Yamagata and Yamanashi) and Kyushu (Fukuoka).

1983

Château Musar

★

GASTON HOCHAR
PROPRIÉTAIRE VITICULTEUR
IMPORTED BY: CHATEAU MUSAR (UK) LIMITED - LONDON

MISE EN BOUTEILLES AU CHÂTEAU   GHAZIR - LIBAN

Lebanon

History: One of the earliest wine making countries,
which had an international reputation for its exports
as early as biblical times.

Current situation: Lebanon has about 50,000 acres
of vineyards, about 75 per cent in the Bekaa Valley.
Wine making is dominated by Serge Hochar who,
despite all the troubles of his war torn country,
usually manages to produces a world class wine. For a
number of years the front line has divided the
vineyards from his winery. Trained in Bordeaux, his
Château Musar (D) is a magnificent blend of
Cabernet Sauvignon, Cinsault and Syrah. It is full
bodied, rich, spicy, full of plummy fruit with a touch
of sweetness and ages wonderfully, reaching its best
after a decade or so. Other producers are now trying
to follow his example.

Grapes: Cabernet Sauvignon, Carignan,
Chardonnay, Cinsault, Muscat, Pinot Noir,
Sauvignan Blanc, Shiraz and Ugni Blanc.

FOURNISSEUR DE LA COUR

Bernard-Massard

BRUT

MÉTHODE TRADITIONNELLE CHAMPENOISE

11%vol.

VIN MOUSSEUX DE QUALITÉ ÉLABORÉ PAR BERNARD MASSARD
A GREVENMACHER · LUXEMBOURG

75cl

Moselle Luxembourgeoise Appellation Contrôlée

CLOS DES ROCHERS

RIESLING 1989

Grevenmacher Fels

75 cl e 11% vol   fût 315
BERNARD-MASSARD, GREVENMACHER, Gd DUCHÉ DU LUXEMBOURG

Luxembourg

History: Formerly part of France, Luxembourg was a
significant wine producer until the French
Revolution. The large vineyard estates were owned
by the church but the land passed to the people after
the Revolution and the vineyards were split up into
tiny holdings.

Current situation: Luxembourg has about 5,000
acres of vineyards, whose average size is less than
three acres, and produces about 12 million litres of
wine a year, mostly light, delicate, fruity whites.
Most of the vineyards are planted along the banks of
the Upper Mosel but generally lower acidity means
they do not mature as well as their German
neighbours.

About 40 per cent of production is exported, mostly
to surrounding countries.

Grapes: Rivaner (Müller Thurgau, which accounts for about half of all plantings), Elbling (about a quarter), Sylvaner, Riesling and Auxerroise. There are small acreages of Gewürztraminer, Pinot Blanc and Pinot Gris.

Classification: There are strict quality laws governing locality, variety, grower, vintage, and wine making. Most wines carry the words 'Vin de la Moselle Luxembourgeoise' but only Appellation Complète (AC) wines are obliged to carry a vintage. Wines carry a neck label awarded by the state controlled Marque Nationale, after tasting and analysis by a panel of experts. Growers must say how much wine they have made and they receive exactly the right number of labels. The Marque is awarded according to the strength of the wine and the categories are: *Non-Admis* (under 12°), *Marque Nationale* (12–13.9°), *Vin Classé* (14–15.9°), *Premier Cru* (16–17.9°), and *Grand Premier Cru* (18–20°)

Regions: *Remich*: Includes Hopertsberg and Wellenstein.

Grevenmacher: Includes Ahn, Bochsberg,
Elderberg, Fels, Gollebour, Keopp, Nussbaum,
Ongkaf, Palmberg, Rosenberg, Troerd, Syrberg and
Wormeldange.
Wintrange: Includes Felsberg, Hommelsberg,
Letschenberg, Remerschen and Schwebsinger.
Stadtbreminus: Includes Dreffert.
Luxembourg City: Includes Bech-Kleinmacher,
Foussach, Greiveldange, Herrenberg, Huette,
Jongerberg, Kreitzberg and Roelschelt.

Styles: *Pinot Gris*: Medium-bodied, with a delicate
bouquet, crisp and fruity. Drink young (3).
Riesling: Lean, elegant and acidic with good fruit.
Will age (3).
Rivaner: Aromatic, light and fruity, with a
suggestion of Muscat. Drink young (3).
Traminer: Can produce big, perfumed, spicy wines.
Will age (4).

Morocco

History: Wine was exported from Morocco to Rome 2,000 years ago, but the country's ancient wine making tradition died out under Moslem rule and was only re-established this century after the influx of French settlers, especially in the 1920s and 1930s.

Current situation: Today there are about 60,000 acres of wine, which has halved since the 1930s as the Government has worked to boost quality. The best wines are red.

Classification: There is a quality system similar to the French *Appellation d'Origine Garantie (AOG)*. Some wines have qualified for it but few use it.

Grapes: The most-planted varieties are Carignan, Cinsault, Grenache and Alicante-Bouschet for reds; Clairette, Macccabeo, Ximénez and Rafsai for whites.

Regions: Fez, Marrakech, Meknes-Fez, Oujda-Berkane and Rabat-Rharb, Casablanca

Styles: *Red*: Blended, medium-bodied, fruity and heady. Drink youngish (C).
Vin gris: pale rosé: crisp, light and fruity. Drink young and chilled (2)
White: Dry to sweet; at best fat and fruity. Drink young (2/4).

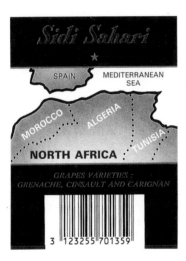

CABERNET SAUVIGNON
HAWKES BAY 1987

Delegat's.

750 ml

12.0%
ALC/VOL

FROM THE CELLARS OF DELEGAT'S WINE ESTATE LIMITED, AUCKLAND.
BOTTLE NO.
LIMITED RELEASE
4177
PRODUCT OF NEW ZEALAND

New Zealand

History: The first vineyard was planted in 1819 by an
Anglican missionary who imported an assortment of
vines from New South Wales. French settlers arriving
in the 1830s brought their native varieties with
them, as did the German immigrants who started to
settle around Nelson in the 1840s. There were
extensive vineyards throughout North and South
Island towards the end of last century but they were
badly hit by disease and by the 1920s the acreage had
fallen to less than 340 acres. Disease, poor weather
and increasing prohibition were all to blame.
Government measures to boost the economy in the
1930s halved imports of wines and rejuvenated the
home industry, and it received a further boost
during the Second World War when almost all
imports dried up.

Current situation: Today there are about 15,000
acres of vineyards, two thirds of them around
Gisborne and Hawkes Bay on North Island. The first
wine was exported in the 1970s and the New Zealand

wine industry hasn't looked back since, its reputation gaining with each new vintage. Overall standards of wine making are very high. Today there are about 11,000 acres of vineyards and the stars are undoubtedly the whites, although at the turn of the century it was the reds that took the medals in international competitions, and they may yet have their day again.

Classification: There are 11 classified areas.

Grapes: *Red*: *Cabernet Sauvignon*: Light, dry and firm with good blackcurrant fruit. Will age (C).
Merlot: Soft, full-bodied and peppery with plummy fruit. Drink youngish (B).
Pinot Noir: Dry, smooth and light with hints of raspberries and good acidity. Drink youngish (B).
Pinotage: Dry and elegant with good fruit and a touch of sweetness. Drink youngish (B).
White: *Chardonnay*: Classic cool-climate Chardonnay. Soft, toasty, buttery and complex fruit. Full-flavoured. Drink youngish, although they age well (2).

Chenin Blanc: Dry, delicate and floral. Drink young (2).

Fumé Blanc: Aromatic, grassy, green, dry and firm. Drink youngish (2).

Gewürztraminer: Dry, perfumed, spicy and floral with exotic fruit flavours. Drink youngish (4).

Müller Thurgau: (the most planted variety) Light, crisp, fresh, floral and grapey. Drink youngish (3).

Riesling: Crisp, delicate, fresh, soft and fruity. Drink young (2/4).

Sauvignon Blanc: Some of the best in the world. Dry, flinty, grassy and aromatic with hints of asparagus and gooseberry, but big, rounded spice and honey finish. Drink young though it ages wonderfully (1).

Sémillon: Fresh, grassy, appley flavours (12).

Areas: *North Island* (N), *South Island* (S)

Aukland (N): Declining vineyard area mostly producing reds.

Bay of Plenty (N): Best for whites, especially Chardonnay and Sauvignon Blanc.

Canterbury (S): Noted for Rhine Riesling, Chardonnay, Pinot Noir and Müller Thurgau.

Gisborne (N): Fertile, high-yielding area, producing mostly whites for cask (box) wines. Can produce good Gewürztraminer and Chardonnay if the weather is kind.

Hawkes Bay (N): Growing acreage producing grapes with good fruit. Müller Thurgau is the main variety, but Cabernet Sauvignon and Merlot produce the best wines.

Marlborough (S): Sunny region with fast-expanding vineyard area. Whites benefit most from a long growing season, especially Sauvignon Blanc. Red wines show promise.

Nelson (S): An area of boutique wineries and skilful wine makers. Chardonnay, Rhine Riesling, Gewürztraminer and Cabernet Sauvignon all show well.

Northland (N)': New wine area of boutique vineyards producing red and white.

Otago (S): Small vineyard area producing mostly whites, especially Müller Thurgau and Rhine Riesling.

Waikato (N): Low yielding area producing good Müller Thurgau, Sauvignon Blanc and Chenin Blanc. Cabernet Sauvignon and Sémillon very promising.

Wairarapa (N): Another new wine area noted for Pinot Noir and Chardonnay but several other varieties produce very good wines.

Portugal

History: Wine was certainly made in Portugal long before the Romans arrived and wine-making has continued virtually uninterrupted since then in the north of the country, although it was outlawed during the Moorish occupation in the south. Portuguese wines were being exported to Britain in the 12th century, and the long trading links between the two countries were established in treaties signed by Edward III, which saw an exchange of British wool for Portuguese wines.

Current situation: Portugal produces about 900 million litres of wine a year from 900,000 acres of vineyards, although exports account for just over 15 million cases, of which three quarters are fortified wines and rosés. Port and Madeira have been the flagship wines of Portugal for centuries but table wines, even the fresh, spritzy Vinho Verde, have been something of lottery. Co-operatives have produced good, everyday wines but have lacked finance and often the will to modernise and raise quality. Higher prices in the rest of Europe, however, sent wine buyers exploring in Portugal and they have discovered some real treasures. There are some very innovative wine makers producing really exciting reds. The first steps have been taken to introduce wine laws. The future looks promising.

Classification: A national wine classification system has been created although it will be some years before it is fully implemented. So far 26 wine producing regions have been designated and given *Indicação de Proveniencia Regulamentada (IPR)* status. When the authorities are satisfied that the wineries are conforming to the laws and there is adequate policing, they will join the small number already granted *Região demarcada (RD)* status, similar to the French AOC.

QUINTA DO
NOVAL
1985
VINTAGE PORT

BOTTLED IN 1987   PRODUCE OF PORTUGAL

This wine is the product of a single vineyard, the famous Quinta do Noval, Pinhão, and is shipped by the proprietors **QUINTA DO NOVAL**, Vinhos, S.A., Vila Nova de Gaia. It should be allowed to mature in bottle for some years, and carefully handled and decanted a few hours before serving

ALC. 20% BY VOL.

Understanding the label

adega	– cellar where wine is made or matured
ano	– year
branco	– white
bruto	– dry (sparkling)
clarete	– light red
Concurso Nacional	– a medal winner in the national wine competition
doce	– sweet
engarrafado	– bottled by
espumante	– sparkling
garrafeira	– slightly stronger table wines, must be aged
generoso	– fortified wine
licoroso	– fortified sweet wine
meio seco	– medium sweet / dry
quinta	– wine estate
região Demarcada	– designated wine region
reserva	– higher quality wines
rosado	– rosé
seco	– dry
tinto	– red
velho	– old
vinho	– wine
vinho de mesa	– blended table wine without any demarcation
vinho Maduro	– aged wine (more than one year old)
Vinho Regionão (VR)	– equivalent to the *French vins de Pays*
Vinho Verde	– young, slightly fizzy white or red

Grapes: *Red*: Baga, Bastardo, Espadeiro Tinto, João de Santarém, Moreto, Tinta Negra Mole, Tinta Pinheira, Tinta Roriz, Touriga Francesa, Touriga Nacional, Vinhão.
White: Alvarinho, Arinto, Avesso, Azal Branco, Boal, Encruzado, Fernão Pires – the most planted white – Loureiro, Malvasia, Moscatel and Verdelho.

Regions: *Alentejo*: A huge region stretching north from the Algarve. Lots of new plantings with classic French varieties. Great potential.
Reds: Big, fruity, rich and robust. Need time and age well (C).
Rosés: Light-bodied and fruity. Drink young (2).
Whites: Aromatic, fresh and fruity with hints of citrus. Drink young (2).

Algarve: The popular coastal strip in the south best known for reds.
Reds: Strong and earthy. Drink youngish (D).

Bairrada: A region of clay soils and rolling hills between the Dão and the coast. Famous for reds and some very good sparkling whites.
Reds: Perfumed with deep intense colour and rich plummy fruit. Soften with age (D).
Whites: Improving. Fresh. crisp and fruity. Drink young (3).

Beiras: In the north of the country with many experimental vineyards and classic varieties. Noted for sparkling wines.
Reds: deep-coloured, strong and acidic. Drink youngish (B).
Whites: Crisp and acidic. Short on fruit. Drink young (2).

Bucelas: Small region of ancient vineyards to the north of Lisbon, noted for whites.
Whites: Improving. Crisp, fresh and dry with good fruit flavours. Drink young (3).

Colares: A sandy, coastal area to the west of Lisbon, noted for reds.
Reds: Massively tannic when young, but soften with age. Violets and cherries on the nose and a peppery, plummy flavour. Lasts for many years (D).

Dao: Very hilly region of about 50,000 acres of vineyards producing mostly reds.
Reds: Big, strong and tannic with full fruit. Age well (D).
Whites: Crisp, fruity, quaffing wine. Drink young (2).

Douro: Less than half the grapes from the Douro valley are used for Port, the rest produce light to full bodied reds, and a wide range of good whites.
Reds: Range in style from light to Burgundian full-blown. Fruity, well made. They age well, and new oak-aged wines have class and great longevity (B).
Whites: Greatly improved. Fresh, fruity, flavourful and exciting Chardonnay. Drink youngish (2).

Oeste: Huge wine area north of Lisbon consisting of five sub-regions – Arruda, Torres, Gaeiras, Alcobaça and Encostas de Aire. Mostly reds.
Reds: Soft with rich cherry fruit. Age well. Good Reservas (B).
Whites: Fresh, buttery and creamy. Drink youngish but can age well (2).

Ribatejo: A large vineyard region straddling the Tagus north east of Lisbon.
Reds: Big and full-bodied, with rich currant fruit. Need time to soften and develop, but keep well (D).
Whites: Improving. Crisp and short on fruit. Drink young (2).

Setubal: Vineyards in the Setubal Peninsula south east of Lisbon, producing exciting reds and whites, many from classic varieties.
Reds: Warm with rich curranty fruit, Cabernet Sauvignon and Merlot being used in blends. Develop well in new oak and age well (C).
Whites: Good early Chardonnay. Fresh, crisp, flowery, fruity Muscats. Drink young (23).

Trás-os-Montes: In the north east corner of Portugal and noted for its rosé (Mateus, etc)
Reds: Light, fruity and acidic to big and heady with cherry fruit. Will age (B/D).
Rosé: Medium-sweet, fruity and often slightly sparkling (4).

Vinho Verde: A large vineyard area running along the coast and inland north of Oporto.
Reds: Very crisp, dry and refreshing. Drink very young (B).
Whites: Fresh and crisp with low alcohol and high acidity. Slightly sparkling. Export wines are often slightly sweetened. Drink very young (4).

Fortified Wines

Carcavelos: A small region close to Estoril and an even smaller production. Only one vineyard produces this dryish, smooth, nutty fortified wine which ages well (D).

Madeira: Part of the Funchal island chain about 375 miles off the Moroccan coast in the Atlantic. Ordinary wines made on the island were literally baked by the sun as they were shipped overseas. The heating up transformed and improved the wines, so the islanders built ovens called '*estufas*' to imitate the process and give Madeira its unique character.

The wines are fermented before baking. Fortification takes place before baking for drier styles; afterwards for greater sweetness.

Their are four styles of Madeira, each named after the grape variety used:

Malmsey: Dark, full-bodied, fragrant and honeyed. Very sweet (9).

Bual: Dark, fragrant and sweet but less cloying because of acidity (7).

Verdhelo: Golden, medium-sweet and nutty. Dries with age (5).

Sercial: Dryish, pale and nutty. Mellow with age (2).

Reserve wines are at least five years old, Special Reserve ten or more, and Exceptional Reserve 15 years or more. Individual vintages must be from a single year and aged for at least 20 years in wood and two in the bottle.

Port

One of the world's great fortified wines made from grapes grown on the slopes of the Upper Douro valley in the north east corner of Portugal. The only region in the world where Port can be grown.

The wine estates (*quintas*) are so steep that the grapes have to be picked by hand. The grapes are pressed and stored in fermenting tanks with the skin and pips for about two days to gain colour and body. The new wine is then drawn off into vats and brandy added. This stops fermentation leaving the port naturally sweet from unfermented grape sugar. The new port spends its first winter in the hills of the Upper Douro before being taken down to the maturation cellars (lodges) at Vila Nova da Gaia, at the mouth of the river opposite Oporto. Here it is tested for quality and characteristics to determine what style of Port it will become.

There are about 50 grape varieties allowed for Port but the best are: Tinta amarela, Tinta barroca, Tinta cão, Tinta roriz, Touriga Francesa and Touriga nacional.

Most Port is aged in wood, which gives it its nutty flavour and it is bottled when ready for drinking. Vintage port is aged in the bottle.

Port styles:

Crusted: Blended from quality Vintages, bottled young and develops sediment in the bottle. Should be decanted (D).

Fine Old Tawny: A blend of young and old wines. Fragrant, smooth and nutty (D).

Fine Old Ruby: Full-bodied, fruity, spicy, luscious and warming (D).

Late Bottled Vintage (LBV): Made from a single harvest, aged for less than six years, smooth, full and rich with harmony between wood and fruit (D).

Ruby: Young port; fruity and sometimes fiery (D).

Old Tawny: Tawny aged for ten, twenty years or more. Soft, creamy and nutty (D).

Vintage: Only produced in the best years. Bottled after two years and aged for ten years minimum. Rich bouquet and warm, rich, spicy fruit. Wonderful (D).

The best vintages come from single estates (Single-Quinta)

Moscatel de Setúbal

A special designation for this lusciously sweet, rich fruit fortified wine made from the Muscat grape. The six year old is usually surprisingly fresh with hints of apricots. There are also twenty year-old and very rare 50 year-olds. Doesn't improve after bottling (8).

Romania

History: There are records of vines being grown in Romania in the 7th century BC, long before the Greeks started to colonise, but it was the Greeks who made them famous by exporting them throughout the civilised world. Wine-making has continued virtually uninterrupted since then.

Current situation: A country with enormous export potential. The Cotnari vineyards in the north are 350 years old. Today, there are more than 750,000 acres of vineyard – a 50 per cent expansion in the past 15 years – and annual production tops 750 million litres, making Romania the largest of all the Eastern European countries, and Europe's sixth largest producer. Most exports still go to Russia, and production has concentrated on sweet white wines. New acreages have been planted with Cabernet Sauvignon, Merlot, Pinot Noir, Chardonnay and Sauvignon Blanc with an eye on exports to the west. Small quantities have already been exported to the

UK and US, and a number of leading shippers are negotiating deals which should increase supplies in 1991 and beyond.

Classification: There is a quality system of sorts modelled roughly on the German system and based on sweetness, natural or otherwise.

Styles: *Cules la Innobilarea Boabelor (CIB)*: Similar to Beerenauslese.
Cules la Maturiate Delpina (CMD): Similar to Splese.
Cules la Maturiate Innobilarea (CMI): Similar to Auslese.
VSO is the lowest quality designation, and *VSOC* the highest.

Regions: Wallachia, Moldavia, Transylvania and Vrancea are the main growing areas. Other areas of promise are Banat, Dobrudja, Murfatlar, Murtenia, Oltenia and Tirnave.

Grapes: Cabernet Sauvignon, Chardonnay, Gewürztraminer, Merlot, Muscat, Pinot Noir, Riesling and Rülander. Feteasca is the best local white, and Babeasca and Feteasca Negra for reds.

Styles: *Cabernet Sauvignon*: Good fruit, full flavour. Well balanced. Will age (D).
Merlot: Delicate and soft with jammy fruit. Easy-drinking. Drink youngish (B).
Pinot Noir: Big and juicy with rich fruit. Drink youngish (B).
Cotnari: Sweet, heady dessert wine. Similar to Tokay. Will age (7).
Riesling: Dry, crisp and fresh with good fruit and acidity. Drink young (3).

South Africa

History: The Cape settlement was established on April 6, 1652 by the Dutch East India Company. The purpose was to supply fresh provisions to the company's vessels rounding the Cape *en route* to the rich trading centres in the Far East. One of the first tasks was to plant vines. The first vineyards were destroyed by raiding Hottentots but they were quickly replanted and the first wine was produced in 1659. In charge of the settlement was Jan van Riebeeck, who realised the value of red wine as a preventative medicine for scurvy among the sailors. For several years, the ships sailing from Europe had orders to transport vines to the settlement and the vineyards' acreage increased, although the grapes were constantly under attack from vast flocks of birds and locust swarms. The settlers realised that the European method of growing vines close together was not working, so they developed new techniques, and experts imported from Europe identified more favourable vineyard sites, which were then planted.

One of the first of these was at Constantia, and the following century their dessert wines had achieved a worldwide reputation. By 1860 wine production topped 4.5 million litres, but exports plunged to only 30,000 litres in 1864 because of high import duties levied in Britain. War and disease hit the industry until 1918 when the wine co-operative KWV was formed, and the vineyard acreage started to increase as the quality of the wines improved.

Current situation: South Africa may have been isolated of late, but with the political climate changing it is set to make an effective return to the world wine scene. The Cape vineyards are among the most beautiful in the world. They enjoy a near perfect climate and produce many outstanding wines which are amazingly good value because of the current exchange rate.

Almost all the vineyards are in the western Cape, fanning out from Cape Town. Today there are about 250,000 acres of vineyards, producing an average 800 million litres of wine a year (950 million in 1989). About 85 per cent of the crop is handled by 70 co-operatives. *Ko-operative Wijnbouwers Vereniging van Zuid-Afrika Beperkt (KWV)* is the central body representing and governing 4,865 grower members. There are 64 estate wineries. Many of the grapes are harvested at night, when it is cool and the grapes have maximum freshness and flavour. Apart from a wide range of table wines, there are good sparkling and fortified wines and grape spirits. A quarter of production is currently exported.

Classification: South Africa has strict Wines of Origin laws, introduced in 1973, and wines which qualify carry the seal attached to the neck of the bottle. Wines are generally classified according to the variety used and the area where they were produced.

How to read the seal:

Blue band indicates the origin of the wine is certified.

Red band guarantees the vintage year.

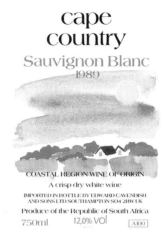

cape country
Sauvignon Blanc
1989

COASTAL REGION WINE OF ORIGIN

A crisp dry white wine

IMPORTED IN BOTTLE BY EDWARD CAVENDISH
AND SONS LTD SOUTHAMPTON SO4 2RW UK

Produce of the Republic of South Africa

750ml   12,0% VOL   A100

Green band certifies that the wine derives from the
stated grape variety.
'*Estate*' certifies it is from one estate identified by
the maker's label.
'*Superior*' (on a gold seal) denotes a wine of superior
quality.
Areas of origin range from single estates to entire
regions, but must always be printed on the label.
There is also an identification number which testifies
that the wine has adhered to the required strict
controls at every stage of production.

Grapes: Most of the vines grown are European
imports, but there are six important hybrids which
were developed locally. The most important of these
is Pinotage for red, while the others – Chenel,
Weldra, Colomine, Grachen and Follet – are all used
for whites.

Reds (local name in brackets): *Cabernet Sauvignon*:
Light-bodied with good balance and good fruit. Age
well (D).
Cinsault (Hermitage): Light to medium-bodied with
rich fruit. Develop well (E).

Merlot: Light-bodied with soft, velvety fruit. Well structured. Age well (B).

Pinotage (a Cape-developed variety): Full, fruity flavour. Age well (B).

Pinot Noir: Good early results. Good fruit and full flavour. Light. Age well (B).

Shiraz: Full-bodied, fruity wines with a smokey character. Age well (D).

Whites (local name in brackets): *Cape Riesling*: Delicate and fruity. In good years it produces great wine (27).

Chardonnay: Impressive early results. Soft and buttery. Age well with oak (2).

Chenin Blanc (Steen): Accounts for a third of all plantings. Produces delicate dry to full, sweet late harvested wines. High acidity and fragrant bouquet. Mellows with bottle age (28).

Clairette Blanche: Delicate, fruity, aromatic when young and often blended (2).

Colombar: Fragrant and fresh, balancing high acid and full fruit. Drink young (2).

Gewürztraminer: Big-flavoured, fruity and spicy with a long finish. Age well (4).

Muscat d'Alexandrie (Hanepoot): Aromatic and mellow with low acidity and Muscat nose (8).

Palomino: Originally grown for distillation. Can make a good varietal in good years if acid and sugar levels are high (2).

Rhine Riesling: High acidity and slight pepperiness. Fruity and well balanced (1/8).

Sauvignon Blanc: Elegant and crisp with a grassy aroma and a full flavour. Long finish (1).

Regions: *Coastal region*: Contains the districts of Constantia, Durbanville, Stellenbosch, Paarl, Tulbagh and Swartland.

Breeriviervallei: Contains the districts of Worcester, Robertson and Swellendam.

Boberg Region: Includes parts of Paarl and Tulbagh but is recognised only for fortified wines.

Seven Districts: A general appellation, covering Overberg, Olifantsrivier, Piketberg, Klein-Karoo, Benede-Oranje (Orange River), Douglas and Andalusia.

Soviet Union

History: Wine making has had a checkered history. Most of the vineyards are concentrated in the south in the republics on or close to the Black Sea and wine making over the centuries has been disrupted depending on the political control of the area. There are still large Moslem populations in the most southern republics. Modern wine making dates from 1950 when the Soviet government launched a massive programme to encourage people to switch from spirits to wine. Between 1950 and 1970 the vineyard acreage doubled and it has doubled again since then.

Current situation: The Soviet Union is set to become the world's largest wine producer. In the last 40 years the vineyard area has increased from less than 1 million acres to more than 3.5 million, and rapid plantings are continuing. Annual production now tops 4,000 million litres – eight times the 1950 level. The Soviet Union imports about 800 million litres of wine per year and exports about 70 million litres. It already has the world's second largest area under vine (after Spain) and is the world's third largest wine producer. It is expected to lead the field in both areas within three or four years. There have been substantial plantings of classic varieties such as Cabernet Merlot, Sauvignon, Aligote and Sauvignon Blanc. About three quarters of the wine produced is sweet and strong although many wineries are concentrating on lighter, dryer wines, partly for home consumption but mainly for export. Unfortunately, the Soviet Union lacks a wine-making infrastructure and the wineries are old. Western investment is needed to modernise both wineries and wine-making ideas. When that has been done, the Soviet Union will become a formidable figure in the export market. Early results, however, have not been encouraging. There are good red and white wines made, but storage and transport seem to cause problems. There are also good sparkling, fortified wines and spirits.

Understanding the label

beloe vino	–	white wine.
krasnoe	–	red.
rozovoe	–	rosé.
desertnoe	–	dessert.
Gruzinskoe	–	Georgian.
shampanskoe	–	sparkling.
stolovoe	–	table wine.
sukhoe	–	dry.
vinozavod	–	winery.

Classification: There is a system of classification operating in most of the republics based on areas of production. The wine laws only govern the area name under which the wine may be sold and the varieties permitted.

Grapes: There are hundreds of local and hybrid varieties grown. The most promising white varieties are Rkatsiteli, Aligoté, Muscat, Riesling, Sémillon, Tokay, Pinot Gris, Riesling and Gurdzhaani. The main reds are: Cabernet Sauvignon, Merlot, Matrassa, Téliani, Mukuzani, Saperavi.

Regions: All the main wine regions are in the south of the Soviet Union, running from Romania in the west along the top of the Black Sea to Georgia in the east and Armenia and Azerbaijan in the south.

Armenia: South of Georgia and bordering Iran and Turkey. This is one of the oldest wine making regions of the world – often called the 'Fatherland of the Vine' – which has specialised in high strength dessert wines and fortified Port- and Sherry-style wines. It produces good brandy and has started to produce promising dry whites and reds.

Azerbaijan: To the east of Armenia, on the borders with Iran. Azerbaijan has a tradition of fortified and very sweet dessert wines made from grapes originally grown for the table. Now the region produces lighter, dryer tables wines, crisp, whites which must be drunk young (2) and attractive, soft, fruity reds, especially from the local Matrassa grape (B). It also produces big, strong, gutsy reds and heady dessert wines.

Georgia: Famous for big, strong, smooth, aged reds, and semi-sweet or sweet whites. An area of great promise. There are now extensive plantings of

Chardonnay, Cabernet Sauvignon and Pinot Noir, mainly to produce wines for export, and there are some wines of potential produced from local varieties such as Saperavi and Mukazani (can be spelt in several different ways) for reds, and Tsinandali for whites. It also produces the best Soviet sparkling wine, some of it using the *méthode champenoise*.

Kazakhstan: Around the north-east edge of the Caspian Sea, this region produces sparkling, fortified and dessert wines. Recent plantings of Riesling vines have produced promising crisp, dry whites.

Moldavia: On the eastern border with, and formerly part of Romania. Formerly known for white and sparkling wines, but there are now extensive plantings of European varieties. It is a very promising area for dry whites (Riesling, Pinot Blanc, Pinot Gris, Aligoté and Muscat), soft fruity reds (Cabernet Sauvignon and Pinot Noir), and good sparkling wines. Fine local reds are made from Saperavi.

Russia: This republic covers the areas around Rostov, on the north east shore of the Black Sea, and is noted for its sparkling wines and Port-type dessert wines. It is now producing reasonable dry reds from Cabernet Sauvignon and Pinot Noir. Stavropol, between the Black Sea and Caspian, is also noted for its heady dessert wines, but is producing promising dry whites from Aligoté Sauvignon Blanc and Riesling. Krasnodar on the eastern shore of the Black Sea produces light table wines – reds from Cabernet Franc and Cabernet Sauvignon, and whites from Aligoté and Riesling. Anapa just to the north, has good Riesling. There are some very promising reds – using Cabernet Sauvignon and Pinot Noir – from around Derbent in the far south in Dagestan, close to the Caspian Sea.

Ukraine: A huge wine-producing area centred around Odessa and Nikolayev on the northern shores of the Black Sea, and around Dniepropetrovsk and Kiyev on the Dnieper which runs north through the centre of the republic. There has been a massive replanting to Cabernet Sauvignon, Pinot Noir, Chardonnay and Riesling and other European varieties. There has been large-volume production of

sparkling wines, but concentration is now on white
and red table wines.

Russian sparkling wine: Russia produces
enormous quantities of sparkling wine, some of it by
the traditional method, but most of it from a system
developed in the Soviet Union called the Russian
Continuous System. The wine is made by being
passed through a series of sealed tanks. Yeast and
sugar are added to start further fermentation, which
produces the bubbles, and then the wine is passed
over oak chips to clarify it before it is pumped into
the next tank ready for bottling.

TORRES ®

Although the noble traditional grapes from our area produce excellent wines, we decided in the early '60s to start in our vineyards a series of experiments with a selection of varieties from the most famous European regions.

Their adaptation to our soil and climate has posed many problems, but we are proud of the result: the old Alsatian vines have produced in our family vineyards a wine of distinctive character, with an enchanting fruitiness and intriguing aromas.

ESTABL⊕ EN 1870

®

Viña Esmeralda ®

PENEDÈS
Denominación de Origen
Produce of Spain

MEDIUM

75 cl e
ALC. 10.5% VOL

BOTTLED BY THE PRODUCER
MIGUEL TORRES, S.A. - VILAFRANCA DEL PENEDÈS - SPAIN

N.° 796-B

Distributed in England & Wales by:
H. SICHEL & SONS LTD. LONDON WC2N 6JP U.K.

Spain

History: The first vineyards were certainly planted more than 3,000 years ago in Andalusia. Phoenician merchants founded Cadiz in about 1100 BC and planted the first vines imported from the eastern Mediterranean. They were followed by the Greeks and the Romans who extended the plantings inland. In the early 8th century when the Arabs invaded there were massive acreages of vineyards and these were maintained for table grapes rather than wine. When Granada, the last bastion of Moorish rule in Spain, was recaptured by the Spanish in 1492, the art of wine making was revived and it has continued ever since. Spain has been exporting wines to Britain since about 1320. The wine industry was badly hit in the 1930s both by disease in the vineyards and declining export markets. It wasn't until the early 1950s that conditions started to improve and the vineyard acreage began to expand again.

Current situation: Spain has made tremendous strides in overall wine quality in the past few years and wines from areas like the huge plain of La Mancha are unrecognisable from the bulk plonk offered a decade or so ago. Better care in the vineyards, new wine making techniques to cope with grapes grown under a blistering sun and improved storage and bottling have all contributed to the improvement.

At the same time, Spain has continued to produce its great wines such as Rioja, Sherry and the sparkling Cavas, with the Penedés and Ribera del Duero heading the growing list of rising stars.

Spain has the world's largest vineyard acreage and is Europe's third largest producer. Each year the harvest yields about 3,000 million litres of wine from 4,250,000 acres of vineyards, almost a quarter of Europe's total vineyard area.

All types of wines are produced, from incredibly fine, bone dry Sherries to big, gutsy long-living reds, and from light, fruity whites to rich dessert.

Classification: *Vinos de la tierra*: Spain's *Vin de Pays* equivalent, although quality varies hugely. Two-thirds of the grapes must come from the region named on the label.
Denominacion de Origen (DO): Applies to nearly two thirds of all Spanish wine production. It governs permitted varieties, yields and methods of wine-making, but generally the DOs cover such large areas that it is no real guarantee of quality. Many excellent producers have still not been awarded DO status.

Understanding the label

abocado	–	medium sweet.
aguja	–	very young spritzy wine.
año ao	–	year.
blanco	–	white.
bodega	–	winery, cellar.
brut	–	dry (sparkling).
brut natur	–	very dry.
cava	–	sparkling wine produced by traditional method.
clarete	–	light red wine.
Comarca Vinícola	–	a designated region.
Con crianza	–	aged wine.
cosecha	–	vintage.
CVC	–	blended from different vintages.
DO	–	a guarantee of the wine's origins.
dulce	–	sweet.
elaborado por	–	made by.
embotellado por	–	bottled by.
espumoso	–	sparkling.
generoso	–	fortified wine.
Gran Reserva	–	a winery's highest quality aged wines.
Granvas	–	sparkling wine produced using the tank method.
jovennuevo	–	young.
Reserva	–	quality aged wines.
rosado	–	rosé.
Sangriá	–	red wine and fruit juice punch.

seco	–	dry.
semi-seco	–	medium dry / sweet.
tinto	–	red.
vendimia	–	harvest.
vino	–	wine.
Vino de la Tierra	–	loosely equivalent to the French Vins de Pays.
vino gasificado	–	sparkling wine produced by adding carbon dioxide.

Grapes: *Red*: *Bobal*: Fruity and low alcohol with intensely deep colour.

Cariñena (Mazuelo in Rioja): Strong and plummy with high tannin. Ages well.

Garnacha Tinta: The most popular red variety. Big, alcoholic, soft and fruity when young. Age well when blended.

Graciano: Declining acreage. Low-yielding, subtle, aromatic and flavourful.

Monastrell: Spain's second most planted red. High-yielding, big, juicy, alcoholic wines. Usually dry.

Tempranillo: Early-ripening, with a distinctive bouquet. Soft and fruity when young. Age well. The main imported red varieties are Cabernet Sauvignon, Malbec, Merlot and Pinot Noir.

White: There are hundreds of different varieties but the major ones are listed below.

Airén: Spain's most planted white. At its best refreshing and tangy with hints of apple and lemon.

Garnacha Blanca: High-yielding with high alcohol and low acidity. Usually blended.

Malvasía: Declining acreages. Big, strong, aromatic and spicy. Ages well.

Moscatel de Málaga: Flowery, aromatic and grapey. Makes dry to rich, sweet wines.

Parellada: Light, fruity, soft and aromatic. Produces still and sparkling.

Verdejo: Soft fruit and zingy acidity. Used for still, sparkling and fortified wines.

Viura (Macabeo): Fresh and fragrant with hints of citrus. Young quaffing wines which age well.

Xarel-lo: Big-bodied and alcoholic. Blended for still and sparkling wines.

The main 'imported' varieties are Chardonnay, Gewürztraminer, Riesling and Sauvignon Blanc.

Regions
North-East:
Alella DO: Small wine producing area north of Barcelona which produces mostly whites.
Reds: Light to medium bodied, soft and fruity. Drink youngish (A).
Rosé: Dry, fresh and crisp with soft fruit. Drink young (2).
Whites: Dry, light and delicate with good acidity to be drunk young; or medium sweet, bigger and richer, to be drunk youngish (25).

Ampurdán-Costa Brava DO: Close to the French border in the Pyrenees, this area mostly produces rosé.
Red: Heavy, full-bodied and fruity. Drink youngish (C). A soft, fruity Beaujolais-style wine, vin novell, is also produced. Drink young (A).
Rosé: Dry, alcoholic, fruity and medium-bodied. Drink very young (2).

White: Light, fruity and medium-sweet. Can be spritzy. Drink very young (4).

Campo de Borja DO: In Aragn, sandwiched between Navarra in the north and Cariñena in the south. Only red and rosé in the DO.
Red: Big, sturdy and alcoholic. Age well. The new-style lighter reds show promise. Drink young (D/C).
Rosé: New-style light and fruity. Drink very young (1).

Cariñena DO: South-east of Rioja, very hot and dry, low yielding and best known for reds.
Red: Big, sturdy. aromatic and fruity. Will age (C).
Rosé: Light and fruity, or big bodied (more like a red). Drink young (24).
White: Light, dry and fruity to big, rich and sweet. Drink young (2/7).

Cava DO: Sparkling wines produced by the Traditional Method, mostly in Catalonia in the hills behind Barcelona. Usually white but some rosé is produced.

Sparkling white: Mostly dry (*extra brutbrut*) but also off dry (*extra seco*), medium dry (*seco*), semi-sweeet (*semi-seco*), and sweet (*dulce*). Quality is usually excellent. Toasty aroma, clean and fresh flavour with good fruit. Drink non-vintage young. Vintage will develop well with age (1/8).

Sparkling rosé: Can be fresh, lively and fruity. Drink young (3).

Conca de Barberá DO: Small, hilly region in the south east of Penedés. Mostly white.

Reds: Often astringent, but can have good fruit. Drink young (C).

Rosé: Dry, light, aromatic and fruity. Drink young (2).

Whites: Clean, fresh and fruity, with hints of lemon. Drink young (3).

Costers del Segre DO: The most westerly of the Catalan DOs, dominated by the Raimat estate where the vineyards have been carved out of the desert. It produces good red and white, using blends of local and imported classic varieties.

Red: Blends produce soft, light wines with ripe blackcurranty fruit. Age well (C).
White: Crisp, fresh and clean. Very good balanced, buttery Chardonnay (2).

Navarra DO: A region producing many fine wines from 65,000 acres of vineyards just to the north of Rioja. Most wine is produced by co-operatives and then sold to *bodegas* for blending. The region has many experimental vineyards and wineries which are all helping to raise quality, and there are some excellent classic variety reds coming on in Ribera Alba (C). Red accounts for half of production, rosé for about 40 per cent and white the remainder. There are five sub-regions:
Baja Montaña: Fresh, fruity, aromatic rosé. Drink young (2).
Ribera Alta:
  Red – Blended, dry, soft and fruity. Drink young (B).
  Rosé – Fresh and smooth. Drink young (2).
  Whites – Light, fruity and quaffable. Drink young (3).

Ribera Baja: Big, full bodied, plummy reds. Age well (D).

Tierra Estella: Light, dry, fruity red and rosé. Drink young (B/2).

   Whites – Dry and crisp with soft fruit.
   Drink young (2).

Valdizarbe: Good value, dry, fruity and aromatic red and rosé. Drink young (B/2).

Penedés DO: The hilly hinterland behind Barcelona and the best wine region in Catalonia. The Torres family has long been the flagship producer although their example has encouraged other growers, and a number now produce outstanding wines, many from classic French grapes.

Red: Ranges from light, dry and fruity (best drunk young) to classic, full-bodied, complex wine with great staying power (B/D).

Rosé: Light and fresh with good fruit. Drink young (2).

White: Ranges from dry to sweet. Light, fruity and aromatic for quick drinking or medium- to full-bodied wine which matures wonderfully in oak (2/7).

Viña

Las Torres

1988

Produced & bottled by
Miguel Torres, s.a.
VILAFRANCA DEL PENEDÉS • SPAIN

11,5% VOL   75 CL   PENEDÉS
                        Denominación de origen   R·796-B

Priorato DO: A hot, dry, mountainous region west of Tarragona. The wines have to be at least 13.5 alcohol to get the DO.
Red: With care it can be good, with raisiny rich fruit and full flavour. Will age (D).
Rosé: Despite the strength it can be fresh and fruity. Drink young (4).

Rioja DO: The Rioja region covers more than 92,000 acres of vineyards to the south-west of Navarra. It produces one of the world's classic wines, although both red and white have undergone changes in recent years. Classic red Rioja (C) smacks of vanilla from oak ageing, with light but sweet fruit, hints of pepper and a smooth richness. Traditional-style Rioja white (2) is wood-aged and develops like white Burgundy. Both age well and reds can last decades in great years.
Some producers have experimented with lighter, less oaky reds, and fresh, steely dry whites with concentrated fruit flavours. Both styles have their place.
Rioja red varieties are Tempranillo – always the major share – Garnacha, Graciano and Mazuelo. White varieties are dominated by Viura and Malvasia.
There are three Rioja districts:
Rioja Alta: The biggest, smoothest Rioja wines with intense fruit.
Rioja Alavesa: The most full bodied; although some lighter styles are appearing.
Rioja Baja: Produces strong, alcoholic wines, usually used in blending.

Styles: *Sin crianzo*: No wood-ageing. Produces light, fruity red and rosé, and crisp, clean, fruity, white, all made to be drunk young (A/1/2).
Crianza: Reds have at least one year in wood, and are usually three years old before being sold. Whites have at least six months wood ageing.
Reserva: Reds are aged for a minimum of three years, at least one of which must be in wood. Whites must have two years ageing. Reserva wines are normally only made in better years and age well, developing softness and complexity.

Gran Reserva: The best wines, aged for at least two years in wood and two in the bottle. Long lasting, complex great wines.

Somontano DO: A new DO in Aragon between the Penedés and Navarra in the Pyrenean foothills.
Red: Light, fragrant and fruity; light- to medium-bodied. Drink young (B).
Rosé: Dry, delicate, light and aromatic. Drink young (2).
White: Light, fruity and sometimes heady. Drink young (3).

Tarragona DO: Coastal vineyards south of Penedés. A big producer of all styles but mostly white.
Red: Big, quaffable and fruity. Drink youngish (C).
Rosé: Dry, light and delicate. Drink very young (2).
White: Medium-bodied, aromatic and fruity. Drink young (3).

Terra Alta DO: Hilly vineyard area inland from Tarragona. Reds are big and strong; whites fresh, fruity but heady; rosés fruity, earthy and heady. All should be drunk young (C/2/2).

North-West

Rias Baixas DO: Vineyards in Galicia on the Atlantic coast north of Portugal.
White: Crisp, clean, fragrant and fruity. Drink young (2).

Ribera del Duero DO: The vineyards follow the valley of the Duero and its tributaries. Vega Sicilia produces one of Spain's finest reds from local and classic varieties. This is not typical of the area but shows what can be achieved.
Red: Light, quaffable and fruity for drinking young; or intense, full-bodied and plummy for ageing. Have great longevity. Cabernet, Malbec or Merlot added to some blends has improved them greatly (C).
Rosé: Light, dry and fruity. Drink young (2).

Ribeiro DO: Winery investment has improved these Galician wines enormously. The wines often have a natural slight fizz.
Red: Light and fruity. Made to be drunk young (B).
Rosé: Delicate, with soft fruit. Drink young (2).

White: Clean, crisp, fresh and fruity. Drink young (2).

Rueda DO: On the Duero, north-west of Madrid and mostly a white producer.
White: Light, fresh and fruity. Mostly drunk young. Can be oak aged (2).

Toro DO: To the west of Rueda and close to the Portuguese border. Noted for reds.
Red: Medium- to full-bodied and tannic with rich fruit. Age well (C).
White: New-style, light, crisp, fresh and fruity. Drink young (2).

Valdeorras DO: Vineyards on the hills around the valley of the river Sil.
Red: Soft with pleasant, good fruit,. Drink youngish (B).
White: Dry, fresh, fruity and aromatic. Drink young (2).

CENTRAL SPAIN
Almansa DO: A small region between the great plateau of La Mansa and the Mediterranean noted for its red and rosé wines.
Red: Big, sturdy, spicy and fruity. Age well, especially in good years (D).
Rosé: Light, fresh and fruity. Drink young (2).

La Mancha DO: Huge amounts have been spent modernising wineries and it shows.
Red: Medium, fruity and easy drinking. Drink youngish (B).
Rosé: Light fresh and very fruity. Drink young (2).
White: Crisp, aromatic and fruity, to rich, full dessert. Drink young (1/7).

Méntrida DO: A small wine producing region to the west of Toledo noted for red and rosé.
Red: Medium- to full-bodied and earthy. Drink young (C).
Rosé: Full-bodied and heady. Drink young (2).

Valdepeñas DO: To the south of La Mancha this region is now producing good reds and much-improved whites and rosés.
Red: Soft with full fruit. Good value. Age well (C).
Rosé: Dry, crisp and fruity. Drink young (2).
White: Light and dry with subtle fruit. Drink young (2).

EASTERN SPAIN

Alicante: The region's vineyards generally lie some way inland in the hills behind the popular coastal resort. Most of the wine is red and high in alcohol.
Red: Big, powerful and high in tannin and alcohol. Age well (D).
Rosé: Dry and heady, more like reds. Drink young (2/C).
Fundillon: A delicious, nutty, heady, aged liqueur from Monastrell grapes (7).

Jumilla: A region of hilly vineyards north of the Segura river, which can suffer years of drought. Most wine is very strong red.
Red: Intense deep colour. Full-flavoured and high alcohol. Drink youngish (D).

Jumilla Monastrell: The best red. Big, fruity and aromatic. Age well (D).
Rosé: Dry, crisp and fruity. Drink very young (2).
White: Improving. Fresh, fruity, aromatic and medium-bodied. Drink young (2).

Utiel Requena: A mountainous region surrounding the two towns after which it is named. Almost all red and rosé.
Red: A high altitude produces soft, fruity, flavoursome wines with hints of herbs. Drink youngish (C).
Rosé: Light, fresh, fragrant and refreshing. Drink young (2).

Valencia: A hugely improved wine producing region climbing into the hills inland from Valencia. The wines are especially popular in the US.
Red: Full, fruity and meaty. Drink youngish though it ages well in oak (C).
Rosé: Soft and fresh, with subtle fruit. Drink young (2).
White: light and crisp, good acidity. Drink young (3).

Yecla: Sandwiched between the DOs of Alicante and Jumilla. A mountainous, stony, chalky region producing mostly red, much of it exported in bulk.
Red: Soft and fruity with high alcohol. Drink youngish (B).
Rosé: Dry and medium-bodied with good fruit and hints of cherries. Drink young (2).
White: Improving. Crisp and fruity. Drink very young (2).

SOUTH WEST
Condado de Huelva: To the north west of the Sherry region; producing mostly white and heady fortified wines – young and dry or sweet and aged.
White: New-style, light, fresh and fruity. Drink young (2).

Málaga: To the north east of the Sherry region; producing wonderful, aged dessert wines ranging from medium-bodied and sweet to treacly-thick and luscious (79).

Montilla-Moriles: An inland area to the north of Malaga, producing whites and an unfortified Sherry-type wine.
White: Light, Amontillado-style (see below) and strong. Nutty, sweet and wood aged (28).

SHERRY
One of the world's great fortified wines and a name that can now only be applied to the produce from the area around Cadiz and Jerez in the south-west corner of Spain. It was a wine well known in Shakespearean England.

The main grape varieties are Palomino, which accounts for more than 90 per cent of production, Pedro Ximénez (PX) and Moscatel Fino. Palomino is the base wine while the other two add sweetness and bouquet.

The secret of Sherry lies in the soil and climate, and the unique way in which it is made. Most of the vineyards are on *albariza* limestone soil which holds moisture, vital for an area prone to severe droughts and baking sunshine.

The grapes are harvested and fermented and the base wine is stored in 500-litre butts. The barrels are not fully filled so that air can mix with the wine and oxidation can take place, the first stage in producing Sherry. Some wine develops a crust formed by '*flor*' – natural yeasts found in the Palomino grape. Wines that do not develop *flor* are fortified with wine spirits straight away, while those that do are carefully classified to determine which style of Sherry they are most suited for, and then fortified accordingly.

Sherry is aged in several tiers of barrels known as a *solera*. Each year up to 30 per cent of the wine in the oldest barrels is drawn off for bottling, and replaced with wine from the next tier, which in turn is topped up with younger wine, and so on. Wine drawn off is sweetened if necessary depending on its style.

The main styles are:
Manzanilla: Pale, dry, delicate and wonderful when newly bottled. Drink chilled (1).

Manzanilla pasada: Older Manzanillo. Stronger, but crisp and fragrant (1).

Fino: Can vary enormously. At best dry and delicate with an appley/almond nose. Drink chilled. Does not keep once bottle opened (2).

Amontillado: An aged Fino. Rounded, mellow, rich and nutty (3).

Oloroso: More highly fortified, with a big bouquet. Complex, rich, fatty and nutty (4/5).

Palo cortado: Rare but wonderful. Very old fino (2/3).

Amoroso/Cream: Sweetened Oloroso created for the British market (6/8).

THE ISLANDS

Canaries: Wines are mostly sold in bulk. Tenerife is the biggest producer, Lanzarote Malvasia the most famous wine. Most wine is still pressed by foot.
Red: Light and fruity, but lacks aroma and depth. Drink very young (B).

Balearics: Mallorca is the biggest producer. A number of experimental vineyards are producing very promising wines with French classic varieties.
Red: Generally light, fruity and strong, but age well in wood in good years (B).
White: Light with low acidity. Must be drunk very young (3).

MERLE DES ROCHES

ERMITAGE DU VALAIS
APPELLATION D'ORIGINE

DOMAINE DU MONT D'OR SION
MISE EN BOUTEILLES A LA PROPRIÉTÉ

SCHWEIZER WEISSWEIN

FENDANT DU VALAIS
APPELLATION D'ORIGINE

*C*aves de Riondaz SA
Sierre

11,5 % vol   1000 ml

Importeur Eimann Marken-Getränke GmbH, Nürnberg

BON PERE GERMANIER-BALAVAUD-VETROZ-VALAIS

Switzerland

History: Wine making can be traced back to Roman times in Valais and Lavaux and in the early 12th century there are records of vineyards tended by Cistercian monks around Lausanne.

Current situation: Landlocked Switzerland in the heart of Europe produces a lot of wine for a small country and drinks most of it so exports are never plentiful. The country has 23 Cantons and every one produces some wine, although French-speaking Switzerland is by far the most important region, accounting for about 28,000 out of the total 35,000 acres. Production averages about 120 million litres a year. Traditionally a white wine country, its volume of red wine production has increased in the last 20 years and now accounts for 40 per cent of production. Quality of reds has also improved, particularly for Pinot Noir and Merlot. The wines are usually expensive, mostly because of difficult production. Many of the vineyards cling precariously

Domaine de
Chauvigny

BEVAIX
appellation Neuchâtel
d'origine

Mis en bouteille au
Domaine E. de Montmollin Fils
Auvernier

to the mountain sides and almost everything has to
be done by hand.

Classification: It has been estimated that there are
about 20,000 different wine labels in Switzerland,
because there is no official classification system to
simplify and regulate matters. Some areas carry
Appellation d'origine, but it means little, while
Geneva now has an *Appellations d'origine*
contrôlée, and Italian speaking Ticini has introduced
the *VITI marque* as an official guarantee of quality.
Some producers state the grape variety used, and
number each bottle. Labels can be written in
German, French or Italian, and the Swiss like to use
terms like '*Premier*' and '*Grand Cru*', but this has
no relation to quality. Labels will name vintage and
producer, however, and if the wine is for export, the
alcoholic strength will be stated.

Grapes: Many grape varieties are grown but the
white Chasselas is by far the most common, followed
by Müller-Thurgau, Johannisberg Riesling,
Malvoisie (Pinot Gris), Gewürztraminer and
Ermitage. Pinot Noir (Blauburgunder), Gamay and
Merlot are the most planted reds.

Regions: *Valois*: In western Switzerland and dominated by the upper Rhône valley. The mountain-side hugging vineyards are noted for light, fresh, fruity whites, often with a little *pétillance*, and are Europe's highest vineyards. There are about 12,500 acres of vineyards and 20,000 owners, of whom only 2 per cent produce their own wine.

Styles: *Dôle AO*: Pinot Noir or Pinot/Gamay blend. Elegant, supple and balanced. Age well (B). *Pinot Noir AO*: Soft and velvety with complex nose and palate. Age well (B). *Fendant AO*: Made from Chasselas. Dry, full-bodied and fleshy with hints of flint and lime blossom. Drink young to youngish (2). *Johannisberg AO*: Made from Sylvaner. Delicate, musky and full. Drink youngish (2). Other wines of interest: *Whites*: Dôle blanche, Ermitage, Amigne, Petite Arvine, Malvoisie, Riesling (all 2/3); *Reds*: Gamay (B), Humagne rouge (B), Syrah (C), Cornalin (C).

Vaud: An area trapped between the Alps to the east and Jura to the west. A classic white area with 80 per

FÉCHY
APPELLATION D'ORIGINE

LES MARTINES
GRAND
VIN DE LA CÔTE
VAUDOISE
❀
EXCLUSIVITÉ HAMMEL SA ROLLE

Illustration originale de Géa Augsbourg &E (c) 1986 by Prolitteris, 8005 Zürich

cent of vineyards planted with Chasselas, which produces a number of different styles of wine, each with its own AO.

Lavaux AO: Harmonious, long and well structured. Drink youngish (2).

La Côte AO: Dry with floral bouquet and lively. Drink youngish (2).

Chablais AO: Dry, exuberant and rich in minerals. Drink youngish (2).

Bonvillars AO: Dry, delicate and lively. Drink young (2).

Salvagnin AO: Made from Gamay and/or Pinot Noir. Fruity, light and supple. Drink youngish (B). Other wines of interest: Pinot Noir (B), Gamay (B), Sylvaner (2) and Pinot Gris (2).

Geneva: On the western tip of Lake Geneva with 3,500 acres of vines. Noted for Chasselas and Gamay.

Gamay de Genève AO: Made from Gamay. Fruity, refreshing and complex. Drink youngish (B).

Perlan AO: Made from Chasselas. Dry, floral and sparkling. Drink young (2).

Other wines of interest: Müller-Thurgau (2/3), Aligote (1/2), Pinot Noir (B).

COLLIVO
TICINO
TENUTA COLLE DEGLI ULIVI
1988
Vino rosso a denominazione di origine prodotto da uve Merlot

Propr. Azienda Agricola Eredi fu B. Caverzasio, Coldrerio
Vinificato e imbottigliato all'origine
Eredi Carlo Tamborini Vini SA, Lamone TI-Svizzera

Neuchâtel and Les Trois Lacs: Hugging the Lakes of Neuchâtel, Bienne and Morat this is the smallest wine district in western Switzerland, noted for surprisingly light, refreshing Chasselas and elegant reds.

Neuchâtel AO: Made from Pinot Noir. Fine, velevety and elegant. Drink youngish (B).

L'Oeil-de-Perdrix: Made from Pinot Noir. A light, fruity, refreshing rosé. Drink young (2).

Neuchâtel AO: Made from Chasselas. Light and crisp with a slight sparkle. Drink young (2).

Other wines of interest: Pinot Gris (2), Chardonnay (2), Müller-Thurgau (2/3).

Ticino: The most southerly Canton. Italian-speaking, and noted for its Merlot.

Merlot del Ticino: DO (*Denominazione di origine*) with a delicate bouquet, and a robust, full flavour. Mellows into delicate, velvety wine. Age well (B). The VITI quality mark is only awarded to wines made exclusively from Merlot which have passed rigorous tasting and analysis

Eastern Switzerland: Includes all 16 German speaking cantons. There are about 5,500 acres of scattered vineyards. The only authorised red variety is Pinot Noir (also known as Blauburgunder and Clevner) and it is often sold under its place of origin. Can be light, fresh and fruity with balanced acidity. Drink youngish (B). White varieties include Chasselas (2), Müller-Thurgau (2/3), Pinot Gris (2) and Gewrztraminer (4).

APPELLATION D'ORIGINE CONTROLEE

Muscat Sec de Kelibia

Vol. Alc.
11°50

75 cl.

Produit et mis en bouteille en Tunisie par U.C.C.V.

Tunisia

History: Vine growing and wine making around Carthage can be traced back to Punic times and was maintained by the Romans. Under Moslem rule, however, all wine-making ceased for more than 1,000 years and it was not revived until the first French settlers arrived in the 1880s and planted new vineyards around Cape Bon and Tunis. The acreage quickly expanded and in 1934 production topped 125 million litres. Two years later, phylloxera struck, and by 1945 the vineyard area had halved and wine production had fallen to less than 40 million litres. A major replanting programme started in the 1950s with many of the classic European varieties imported.

Current situation: There are now about 75,000 acres of vineyards and annual production is around 90 million litres. The industry is not organised and the best wines are the sweet Muscats, although soft fruity reds similar to Provence wines are produced.

Classification: There are loose quality laws based on the French; with *Vins de Consommation Courante (VCC)*, *Vins Supérieurs (VS)*, *Vins de Qualité Supérieure (VDQS)*, and *Appellation d'Origine Contrôlée (AOC)*.

Grapes: *Reds*: Carignan, Cinsault, Mourvèdre, Alicante-Bouschet, Pinot Noir, Cabernet Sauvignon and Cabernet Franc.
Whites: Muscat, Beldi, Clairette de Provence, Ugni Blanc, Pedro Ximénez, Sémillon and Sauvignon Blanc.

Regions: All the main producing regions are in the coastal belt: Bizerte-Mateur-Tebourba, Grombalia, Kelibia-Cap Bon and Thibar.

Styles: *Red*: Can be soft and fruity, but oxidise if not drunk young (B).
Rosé: Can be light, crisp and fruity but must be drunk very young (2).
White: Spicy, dry Muscat and some promising dry blends (2).
Muscat: Rich, sweet, almost honeyed dessert wines (8).

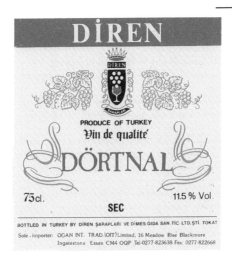

DİREN

PRODUCE OF TURKEY

Vin de qualité

DÖRTNAL

75 cl.   11.5 % Vol.

SEC

BOTTLED IN TURKEY BY DİREN ŞARAPLARI VE DİMES GIDA SAN. TİC. LTD. ŞTİ. TOKAT
Sole Importer: OGAN INT. TRAD.(OIT) Limited, 16 Meadow Rise Blackmore
Ingatestone Essex CM4 OQP Tel:0277-823638 Fax: 0277-822668

Turkey

History: Grapes have been grown in Turkey for
thousands of years and wild varieties were common
along the coast and in Anatolia. There are records of
wine-making dating back to 3,000 BC and the
tradition continued until the Middle Ages when the
Turks became Moslems and alcohol was banned.
Grapes were still produced, but only for the table.
Wine-making started again in the mid 19th century
when almost all was exported. Production in the late
19th century reached 350 million litres. Turkey was
still a major wine exporter at the turn of the century
but the industry virtually collapsed in the 1920s and
1930s. Replanting the vineyards started in earnest in
the late 1930s under the control of the state
monopoly wine organisation.

Current situation: Since 1940, vineyard acreage
has steadily grown to about 2 million acres and
Turkey now has the fifth largest area under vine,
although most grapes are for the table or dried fruit.
Wine production is about 40 million litres a year,
about 10 per cent of which is exported.

Grapes: There are said to be more than 1,000 grape varieties in Turkey, but the most promising varieties are:

Red: Gamay, Pinot Noir, Cinsault, Carignan, Grenache, Merlot, Alicante-Bouschet, Cabernet Sauvignon

White: Smillon, Riesling, Muscat, Chardonnay, Clairette, Yapincik, Vasilaki, Bornava Misketi.

Regions: Aegean, Anatolia (the best producer), Ankara, Black Sea Coast, Mediterranean Coast and Thrace-Marmara (which shows great promise).

Styles: *Red*: There are some attractive, light, fruity reds made from Gamay; and some good medium-bodied blends using Cinsault, Carignan and Grenache (BC).

White: Usually flabby but reasonable dry with crisp Smillon and some early attempts at blends of traditional and European varieties (2). Local wines tend to be heady and oxidised and range from off dry to sweet.

Dessert: Big, heady Muscat and Muscatels, often oxidised and too old (8).

1984
Napa Valley
CABERNET SAUVIGNON
ALCOHOL 12.5% BY VOLUME
PRODUCED AND BOTTLED BY
ROBERT MONDAVI WINERY
OAKVILLE, CALIFORNIA

United States
of America

History and Current Situation: Most states in the US produce wine, but California outproduces them all. The vineyards of California produce about 96 per cent of the country's total wine production, with New York State and Washington State accounting for just under two per cent each. Of the other wine states Arkansas, Michigan, Missouri, Ohio and Pennsylvania are the most important, although production is tiny. Wine is never likely to be made in Alaska but it is possible for every other state to have a vineyard or two some day, even if for only curiosity's sake. Florida now has a handful of vineyards despite its tropical climate; Hawaii has had vineyards for almost 180 years, and North Carolina's single vineyard is producing very acceptable but expensive Cabernet Sauvignon and Chardonnay wines. Many states have great potential; for example Oregon, and Washington, which now has more than 200

vineyards, many producing excellent wines.
The west coast generally produces better wines,
because vineyards on the Atlantic seaboard,
especially New York State, have relied on local
varieties, Lambrusco and others. All this is changing,
with classic European varieties taking over and many
promising wines being made as a result. Virginia
produces very classy Chardonnay, for instance.
Wine-making in the US has taken a lot from Europe,
including grape varieties and many of the old
established names to describe the style of wine; for
example Chablis, Claret and Hoch. The United
States has given the world a totally different
approach to wine-making. Wine-makers have not
been restricted by the traditions demanded in
Europe. Instead, they have been free to experiment
and innovate, they have had the resources to build
the world's finest and most modern wineries, and
many have proved to be the equal of the best wine
makers anywhere.
The anti-alcohol lobby and increased interest in diet
and health persuaded the wine makers to produce
low-alcohol wines and coolers, but these are not
really wines in the strict sense.

1985
NAPA VALLEY
CABERNET SAUVIGNON
ALCOHOL 13½% BY VOLUME
PRODUCED AND BOTTLED IN OUR CELLAR BY
HEITZ WINE CELLARS
ST. HELENA, CA, U.S.A. CONTAINS SULFITES

The United States has about one million acres under vine, yielding an average 2,000 million litres of wine a year. Exports are steadily increasing, especially for medium- and top-quality wines.

Classification: Each state has its own appellation of origin, but there are a number of other categories. *American Wine* or *Vin de table* is generally blended wine and can come from one or more areas in the US. If a wine comes from two or three neighbouring states (*Multi-State Appellation*), the percentage from each must be shown on the label. There are also State and County Appellations, for which at least 75 per cent of the grapes must come from the designated area.

The *Bureau of Alcohol, Tobacco and Firearms (BATF)*, which is part of the Federal Department of Treasury, designates and polices about one hundred *Approved Viticultural Areas*. To qualify, the area must have a proven reputation for quality, defined boundaries and specific characteristics (soil, climate, physiology, etc.) to distinguish it from other areas. 85 per cent of the grapes used must come from there. When an individual vineyard is named, 95 per cent of the grapes must have been grown there.

The AVAs cover only areas of production and like the French AOCs are not necessarily a guide to quality. For tax purposes a table wine must be between ten and fourteen per cent alcohol, so some big, beefy reds fall outside this category although they are still 'table wines' in every sense. Dessert wines between 17 and 21 per cent are judged by alcohol, not sweetness, so a Trockenbeerenauslese-style wine may be a table wine, while that big, thumping, bone dry red may be a dessert wine!

US wines can also be sold by variety, by generic name (Chablis or Loire) to denote a blend, or by upmarket trade names, such as the famous Opus One. Generic names such as those above are banned on exports to the EC.

If a vintage is given, 95 per cent of the wine must be from that year.

Grapes: North America has many local grape varieties belonging to the Labrusca family. Many vineyards, especially those in the eastern half of the country, still use them for wine, but imported classic European varieties produce the best wines, with the exception of the native Zinfandel which produces excellent light reds.

Styles: *Red*: *Barbera*: Usually used for blending, but it produces big, tart, fruity reds which age well (D). *Cabernet Sauvignon*: Big, oaky wines have given way to elegant, lighter styles, full of rich, curranty fruit and flavour. Sensible oak ageing and a little blending with Merlot have done wonders. Drink youngish although the best wines age well (D). *Carignan*: Often blended, but it produces big, gutsy varietals which will age (E). *Gamay*: Light, fresh and fruity for quick drinking; or bigger style with more tannin and wood ageing. Drink youngish (B/C). *Grenache*: Produces light, aromatic, fruity reds and full-flavoured rosé, which is off-dry to medium. Drink young (C/2).

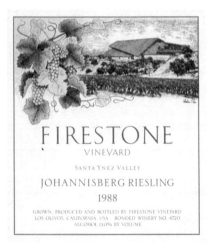

FIRESTONE
VINEYARD

SANTA YNEZ VALLEY

JOHANNISBERG RIESLING

1988

GROWN, PRODUCED AND BOTTLED BY FIRESTONE VINEYARD
LOS OLIVOS, CALIFORNIA, USA · BONDED WINERY NO. 4720
ALCOHOL 11.0% BY VOLUME

ROBERT MONDAVI WOODBRIDGE.

1988

California

WHITE ZINFANDEL

PRODUCED AND BOTTLED BY ROBERT MONDAVI WINERY
WOODBRIDGE, CALIFORNIA, PRODUCE OF USA, ALC. 10% BY VOL.

Merlot: Acreage is fast expanding. Often blended, but it produces a soft, plummy, velvety fruit varietal. Drink youngish, but it will age (B).

Petit Syrah: Often blended, but it produces dark, big, peppery, ripe fruit wine, which will age (D).

Pinot Noir: Most goes for sparkling wine, but it produces light, aromatic, tart wines with curranty fruit, Drink youngish (B).

Zinfandel: Used for quick-drinking rosé (white Zinfandel), which is Beaujolais-like, light and fruity (2), or big, peppery, rich fruited reds which age well (D). Also used for dessert and sparkling wines.

White: *Chardonnay*: Classy, fruity and full of flavour, ranging from crisp to fat and buttery. New style is for lighter, elegant wines, rather than too much oak. Drink the lighter styles youngish; but the oak-aged will last (2/3).

Chenin Blanc: Improving, with better fruit and acidity. Honeyed. Drink youngish (3).

Colombard: (most planted white): Clean, crisp, fruity varietal. Drink young (3).

Gewürztraminer: The best are dry and need bottle age to bring out bouquet and flavour. Most is made off-dry to medium for drinking young (4).

Muscat Blanc: Light-style, perfumed and flowery. Off-dry to dessert. Drink young (3/8).

Riesling: Usually crisp, off-dry, spicy, fruity and medium-bodied. Otherwise lusciously sweet. Drink youngish, although sweeter styles have more staying power (3/7).

Sauvignon Blanc (Fumé Blanc): Fresh and grassy with hints of melon and asparagus. Will last but drink youngish (1).

Sémillon: Very promising, crisp, dry and herbacious, or lusciously sweet if grapes are picked late. Drink young although it can be wood aged (2/7).

Regions and Styles:
California

Wine making was introduced by Catholic missionaries in the 1770s, and although some wineries have a long pedigree, the main surge has been in the past two or three decades, when the number of wineries rose fivefold to about 600. In the same time, the vineyard acreage has more than doubled to about 330,000 acres today.

The main AVAs are: Alexander Valley, Anderson Valley, Arroya Seco, lmedo County, Amador County, Los Carneros, Chalone, Clear Lake, Dry Creek Valley, Edna Valley, El Dorado, Livermore Valley, Mendocino County, Monterey County, Napa Valley, Paso Robles, Russian River Valley, San Joaquin Valley, San Luis Obispo, Santa Barbara County, Santa Cruz, Santa Ynez, Santa Maria, Sonoma County, Stag's Leap District and Temecula.

Napa Valley: The principle wine region in the United States and the birthplace of wine-making in California. The valley is a couple of hours' drive north of San Francisco and is between three and four miles wide and 30 miles long, running just to the north of St.Helena. Vines cover almost all the arable land. The climate and soil are near-ideal for regularly producing big crops of good quality grapes. Flavour is the keynote of Californian wines and the ultra-modern wineries are able to develop this to the full.

Cabernet Sauvignon: Rich, with ripe currant fruit, and flavour-packed. Will age (C).

Pinot Noir: Soft and fragrant with plum fruit. Light to big and rich. Age well (B).
Zinfandel: Either young, fun and fruity, or big, powerful and peppery. Will age (D).
Chardonnay: Lighter-style, fresh, soft and buttery, with complex flavours. Become drier with smokey, toasty flavours when wood aged (2).
Fumé Blanc (Sauvignon): Light and crisp with hints of gooseberries. Drink young (1).
Riesling: The best are sweet, with big acidity to balance. Will age (6/8).

Sonoma Valley: Containing many famous wineries, this was where the first imported European varieties were planted. Russian emigrés are reputed to have planted the first vines between 1810 and 1820, however, which is why much of this north coast wine region is still referred to as Russian River.
The main varieties are Cabernet Sauvignon, Pinot Noir, Zinfandel and Gewürztraminer. The temperature is slightly cooler than in the Napa and the vineyards can produce wines with far more subtle flavour and bouquet.

Other States:
Arkansas: An area of great promise, with good Cabernet Sauvignon (D).
Idaho: Acreage is increasing. Produces good whites with good fruit and high acidity, especially Chardonnay, Riesling and Gewürztraminer.
Maryland: An expanding acreage, concentrating on Cabernet Sauvignon (D) for red; Chardonnay (2) and Riesling (4) for white. Produces fine reds.
New Mexico: Producing good whites, especially Chardonnay (2), Sauvignon Blanc (1) and Chenin Blanc (3).
New England: There are wineries throughout the New England states, producing mostly whites, especially Chardonnay (2), Riesling (3/4), Gewürztraminer (4) and Sauvignon Blanc (1).
New York State: Traditional local varieties are on their way out, and new, classic European vines very much in. The transformation has been tremendous. Good varietals are now being produced from Merlot

(B) and Cabernet Sauvignon (4), Chardonnay (2), Riesling (4), Gewürztraminer (4) and Sauvignon Blanc (1).

Oregon: The cooler climate and higher-altitude vineyards offer great potential. Produces light, delicate Pinot Noir (B), promising light, fruity Cabernet Sauvignon (D), and good Chardonnay (2), Gewrztraminer (4) and Riesling (3/4). Pinot Gris (2) shows great promise.

The main wine-producing areas are: Columbia, Umpqua and Willamette Valleys.

Texas: A new industry with a growing acreage. Good Sauvignon Blanc (1) and Chenin Blanc (3), improving Chardonnay (2), Riesling (3/4) and Gewürztraminer (4). Reds are mainly Cabernet Sauvignon (D), Merlot (B), Pinot Noir (B) and Zinfandel (D).

Washington: Another young industry that has catapulted into the wine headlines for both red and whites. The Cascades split the state in two with the cool wet Puget Sound basin in the west and the warm, dry Columbia River basin in the east. Most of the wineries are in the east producing high quality Chardonnay (2), Riesling (3/4) and Sémillon ($2\frac{1}{2}$); and wonderfully fruity Cabernet Sauvignon (D) and Merlot (B). The main regions are Columbia Valley AVA, Walla Walla Valley AVA and Yakima Valley.

Uruguay

History: The first vines were planted in the 1890s around Montevideo and vines were imported mainly from France and Italy. Harriague, the most planted variety, is thought to stem from the Madiran from south west France. Barbera and Nebbiolo were imported from Italy.

Current situation: A small country but a big producer. The 55,000 acres of vineyards produce about 100 million litres of wine a year, most of it drink at home. All styles are produced from drinkable red and white table wines, very deep rosé, sparkling, dessert and fortified. Some good Cabernet Sauvignon is being produced and there are efforts to secure export markets.

Grapes: Harriague, Vidiella and Cabernet Sauvignon for red, usually blended; and Sémillon, Pinot Blanc, Riesling and Pedro Ximénez for white. There have been substantial plantings of other imported varieties in recent years, especially Cabernet Franc, Pinot Noir, Merlot, Barbera, Nebbiolo and American hybrids.

Regions: The main vineyards are planted on the rolling volcanic hills inland of Montevideo in the south, in the central region of Florida, and in a strip close to the border with Argentina. The main regions are: Montevideo, Canelones, Florida, Maldonado, Montevideo, Paysandu, San Jose and Soriano.

Styles: Most wines are blended and the introduction of hybrids is lowering quality. Most promise is shown by varietals such as Sémillon (2), Riesling (2) and Cabernet Sauvignon (D). Cabernet Sauvignon/Vidiella blends produce very soft, fruity attractive reds (C).

Yugoslavia

History: Wine-making dates back 4,000 years and the first vines were probably imported from Thrace. Wine making continued under the Greeks and Romans and was largely controlled by the Church during the Middle Ages. Turkish domination of much of the country meant an end to wine production until the 19th century. The northern part of the country, especially Ljutomer, was part of Austria and its wine making traditions still reflect this. Until quite recently, many of the wines from northern Yugoslavia were sold with Germanic names and they achieved considerable export successes.

Current situation: There are more than 250,000 acres of vineyard and annual production is about 650 million litres, although yields have been hit in the past four or five years. Yugoslavia is the world's tenth largest wine producer and about 25 per cent of production is exported.

Traditionally, the country is a producer of heady, beefy reds and strong whites. The best indication of the strength of local reds is that even the locals dilute them. Exports to the west were built on Laski Riesling (now called Rizling), but Yugoslavia is now concentrating on producing quality varietals, especially Cabernet Sauvignon, Merlot and Pinot Noir. Imported varieties like Gewürztraminer, Traminer, Pinot Gris, Pinot Blanc, Rhein Riesling and Sauvignon Blanc all show promise.

Classification: New laws have been introduced to try to control the quality of wines for export although they are in their early days. Anxious to win hard currency, however, the wine makers realise that quality must be raised and new lighter-style wines produced. Yugoslavia has great potential if the wine industry can fund the necessary modernisation programme, and the wine makers can overcome problems of storage and oxidation.

Grapes: There are many local varieties, but few offer much export potential, other than Vranac,

Malvazÿa, Mali Plavac and Teran. The imported varieties listed above offer the greatest potential for both varietals and blends.

Regions: The two main producing regions stretch the length of the country, hugging the Adriatic coastal strip or following the central plain and foothills that run down the middle of the country.
The Coastal Strip Croatia: Produces big, gutsy reds from the local Plavac grape (D) and lighter style, fruitier reds from the Teran variety (2).
Slovenia: Produces mostly reds, and is famous for the rich Kraski Teran, strong in minerals and allegedly possessed of curative properties (D).
Herzegovina: Produces big, rich, perfumed whites (2), and heady reds. An area of potential, with increasing plantings of European varieties.
Montenegro: Produces pleasant, easy-drinking, fruity reds from the Vranac grape (B).

The Central Region Inland Croatia: Produces good varietal whites from Traminer, Sémillon, Pinot Blanc, Sauvignon Blanc and Riesling. Good, varietal wines with fragrance, balance and flavour.

MILION YUGOSLAV

Gewurztraminer

Kvalitetno Vino–QUALITY WINE

MEDIUM DRY
Fruska Gora

1 litre e   12%Vol

Kosovo: Produces red and white, dry to sweet specially tailored for the German market.

Macedonia: Replanted since 1950. mostly with local varieties, and now being replanted with classic European varieties. Good reds from Vranac (B). An area of good potential.

Serbia: (the largest wine producing area); Good blended reds from Gamay / Pinot Noir (B).

Slovenia: Most famous for Ljotomer Riesling, which is light and fruity with crisp acidity (4). Also produces good, dry, crisp, fruity whites from Sauvignon Blanc, and rich, fruity, light Cabernet Sauvignon (C).

Voivodina: Produces mostly fruity, dry to medium-sweet white (25), and promising soft, fruity Merlot (B).

Styles: *Vranac*: Big, rich and robust. Ages well (D).
Cabernet Sauvignon: Rich fruit and quite tannic. Needs time to mellow (D).
Laski Rizling: At its best, aromatic, rich and fruity, but variable. Drink young (4).
Gewürztraminer: Fragrant, spicy, fruity and attractive style. Drink young (4).
Other wines to look out for: Traminer, Pinot Blanc, Merlot and Pinot Noir.

IHPA 521

FLAME LILY
SPARKLING WHITE WINE
BRUT

Bottled at Mukuyu Winery for Philips Central Cellars, Harare.
Selected and shipped by Vinceremos Limited, Leeds, LS6 2LQ, UK.

75cl   PRODUCE OF ZIMBABWE   11.5% vol.

Zimbabwe

Current Situation: A tiny but expanding producer whose wines have curiosity value now but show promise. There are less than 2,000 acres of vineyards, but they are increasing. The vineyards are at altitude to benefit from the cooler climate, and the handful of producers have started to export a small part of the annual 2 million litre production.

Grapes: Cabernet Sauvigon, Chenin Blanc, Cinsault, Clairette Blanche, Colombard, Hanepoot, Muscatel, Muscat d'Hambourg, Pinotage, Riesling, Seneca and Servan Blanc.

Regions: Bulawayo, Gweru, Harare and Mutare.

NUMBER CODE

10 Exceptional
 9 Outstanding
 8 Very good
 7 Good
 6 Above average
 5 Average
 4 Below Average
(*for charts overleaf*)

Vintage Chart – White

	1990*	1989	1988	1987	1986	1985	1984	1983	1982	1981	
Australia	7	7	8	8	9	8	7	7	8	8	
Austria	8	9	8	8	8	9	8	9	7	7	
Bulgaria	9	7	8	–	–	–	9	–	–	–	
Chile	8	8	8	7	7	7	8	7	7	6	
England	9	9	6	6	7	8	7	8	8	7	
Bordeaux	8	8	9	7	9	7	6	8	6	6	FRANCE
Burgundy	9	7	8	7	9	8	7	6	8	7	
Champagne	8	8	7	7	7	9	5	9	8	8	
Loire	8	9	9	6	7	9	5	8	6	6	
Rhone	8	9	8	8	7	8	7	9	8	7	
Mosel-Saar	8	9	9	8	7	9	6	9	5	6	GERMANY
Nahe	9	9	8	7	8	8	5	9	6	6	
Rhine	9	9	8	7	7	8	5	9	6	6	
Italy	8	7	8	6	8	9	4	7	8	7	
New Zealand	9	9	9	9	9	8	7	8	7	8	
South Africa	8	7	8	8	7	7	6	6	7	8	
Spain	8	7	8	7	7	8	7	7	7	8	
U.S.A.	8	8	7	9	9	9	9	8	7	8	

*Provisional

Vintage Chart - Red

1990	1989	1988	1987	1986	1985	1984	1983	1982	1981	
8	8	8	7	8	7	8	–	–	–	Argentina
8	6	8	8	8	8	8	7	8	7	Australia
10	7	8	7	9	8	9	7	6	8	Bulgaria
9	8	8.	8	8	8	8	8	7	7	Chile
8	8	8	6	8	8	5	9	9	7	Bordeaux
9	8	9	7	7	9	5	7	6	4	Burgundy
8	9	8	6	8	9	7	8	7	6	Loire
8	7	8	6	7	9	7	9	8	6	Rhone
9	9	7	6	8	10	7	7	10	5	Piedmont
9	7	9	7	7	10	5	9	8	7	Tuscany
7	6	9	4	8	9	5	9	6	9	Veneto
8	8	7	7	8	9	8	7	–	–	New Zealand
8	7	6	6	5	9	6	9	6	5	Portugal
9	7	8	8	8	6	6	6	8	6	South Africa
8	7	6	8	8	8	6	7	9	8	Spain
8	7	7	8	9	10	8	7	7	6	U.S.A.

FRANCE } (Bordeaux, Burgundy, Loire, Rhone)

ITALY } (Piedmont, Tuscany, Veneto)

White Rosé & Sparkling

	Algeria	Argentina	Australia	Austria	Brazil	Bulgaria	Canada
crisp, dry	✓	✓	✓	✓	✓	✓	✓
aromatic dry	✓	✓	✓	✓	✓	✓	✓
medium			✓	✓	✓	✓	✓
sweet	✓		✓	✓		✓	✓
v. sweet	✓	✓	✓	✓		✓	
Aged oaky			✓			✓	
Aged unoaked			✓			✓	
Aligoté			✓			✓	✓
Chardonnay		✓	✓	✓	✓	✓	✓
Chenin Blanc		✓	✓		✓	✓	✓
Gewürztraminer			✓	✓		✓	✓
Müller-Thurgau			✓	✓			
Muscat	✓	✓	✓		✓	✓	
Riesling		✓	✓	✓	✓	✓	✓
Sauvignon Blanc			✓	✓		✓	✓
Sémillon			✓	✓			
ROSÉ Dry	✓		✓			✓	✓
ROSÉ Medium			✓				
ROSÉ Sparkling		✓	✓			✓	✓

Chile	China	Cyprus	Czechoslovakia	England	Bordeaux	Burgundy	Loire	Rhone	Others	Germany
					FRANCE					
✓	✓	✓	✓	✓	✓	✓	✓	✓	✓	✓
✓	✓	✓	✓	✓	✓	✓	✓	✓	✓	✓
		✓	✓	✓	✓		✓	✓	✓	✓
	✓	✓	✓	✓	✓				✓	✓
		✓	✓		✓		✓		✓	✓
		✓	✓	✓	✓	✓			✓	✓
		✓	✓	✓	✓	✓			✓	✓
✓	✓	✓			✓	✓				
						✓				
			✓							
			✓	✓						✓
			✓					✓		
	✓	✓	✓							✓
✓			✓		✓		✓			
✓										
		✓		✓	✓	✓	✓	✓	✓	✓
		✓		✓				✓	✓	✓
✓				✓		✓	✓	✓	✓	✓

White Rosé & Sparkling	Greece	Hungary	India	Israel	Italy	Japan	Lebanon
crisp, dry	✓	✓	✓	✓	✓	✓	
aromatic dry	✓	✓	✓	✓	✓	✓	✓
medium	✓	✓		✓	✓	✓	✓
sweet	✓	✓	✓	✓	✓		✓
v. sweet	✓	✓		✓	✓		✓
Aged oaky	✓	✓		✓	✓		
Aged unoaked		✓		✓	✓		
Aligoté					✓		
Chardonnay	✓	✓	✓	✓			
Chenin Blanc				✓		✓	✓
Gewürztraminer					✓		
Müller-Thurgau		✓					
Muscat	✓				✓		
Riesling		✓		✓	✓	✓	✓
Sauvignon Blanc	✓	✓		✓	✓	✓	
Sémillon					✓	✓	✓
ROSÉ Dry	✓	✓		✓	✓		
ROSÉ Medium		✓		✓	✓		
ROSÉ Sparkling		✓	✓	✓	✓		

Luxembourg	Morocco	New Zealand	Portugal	Romania	South Africa	Soviet Union	Spain	Switzerland	Tunisia	Turkey
✓	✓	✓	✓	✓	✓		✓	✓	✓	✓
✓	✓	✓	✓	✓	✓	✓	✓	✓	✓	✓
✓	✓	✓	✓	✓	✓	✓	✓	✓	✓	✓
	✓	✓	✓		✓	✓	✓		✓	✓
	✓		✓		✓	✓	✓		✓	✓
		✓	✓	✓	✓	✓	✓			
		✓	✓	✓	✓	✓	✓			
						✓	✓			
		✓	✓	✓	✓	✓	✓			✓
		✓			✓					
✓		✓		✓	✓			✓		
✓		✓						✓		
			✓	✓	✓	✓			✓	✓
✓		✓	✓	✓	✓	✓		✓		✓
		✓	✓		✓		✓		✓	
		✓	✓			✓	✓		✓	✓
	✓		✓		✓		✓	✓	✓	
	✓		✓		✓	✓	✓	✓	✓	
		✓	✓		✓	✓	✓			

White Rosé & Sparkling	Uruguay	U.S.A.	Yugoslavia	Zimbabwe
crisp, dry		✔	✔	✔
aromatic dry	✔	✔	✔	✔
medium	✔	✔	✔	✔
sweet	✔	✔	✔	✔
v. sweet		✔	✔	
Aged oaky		✔		
Aged unoaked		✔		
Aligoté				
Chardonnay		✔		
Chenin Blanc		✔		✔
Gewürztraminer		✔	✔	
Müller-Thurgau				
Muscat		✔	✔	✔
Riesling	✔	✔	✔	✔
Sauvignon Blanc		✔	✔	
Sémillon	✔	✔	✔	
ROSÉ Dry		✔		
ROSÉ Medium		✔		✔
ROSÉ Sparkling		✔		✔

Syrah	Pinot Noir	Merlot	Gamay	Cabernet Sauvignon	full-bodied	medium-bodied	off-dry	Country wines	Bordeaux-style	Light dry	
√	√		√	√	√						Algeria
		√		√					√	√	Argentina
√	√	√	√	√	√	√	√	√	√	√	Australia
	√	√		√					√	√	Austria
	√	√		√	√				√	√	Brazil
	√	√		√	√	√	√	√	√	√	Bulgaria
	√		√	√				√	√	√	Canada
	√			√		√	√	√		√	Chile
				√						√	China
				√		√	√	√	√	√	Cyprus
				√		√	√	√	√	√	Czechoslovakia
	√									√	England
		√		√				√	√	√	Bordeaux
	√					√	√	√		√	Burgundy
	√		√	√				√		√	Loire
√						√	√	√	√	√	Rhone
√	√	√	√	√		√	√	√	√	√	Others
										√	Germany
				√	√				√	√	Greece
√	√	√		√	√	√	√	√		√	Hungary

FRANCE *(Bordeaux, Burgundy, Loire, Rhone, Others)*

Syrah	Pinot Noir	Merlot	Gamay	Cabernet Sauvignon	full-bodied	medium-bodied	off-dry	Country wines	Bordeaux-style	Light dry	
	✓			✓						✓	India
	✓	✓		✓	✓	✓	✓	✓		✓	Israel
	✓	✓		✓	✓	✓	✓	✓		✓	Italy
		✓		✓		✓			✓	✓	Japan
✓	✓			✓	✓	✓					Lebanon
										✓	Luxembourg
						✓					Morocco
	✓	✓		✓		✓	✓			✓	New Zealand
	✓	✓		✓	✓	✓	✓	✓		✓	Portugal
	✓	✓		✓	✓	✓		✓	✓	✓	Romania
✓	✓			✓	✓	✓	✓	✓	✓	✓	South Africa
	✓	✓		✓	✓	✓		✓			Soviet Union
	✓	✓		✓	✓	✓	✓	✓		✓	Spain
	✓	✓	✓					✓		✓	Switzerland
	✓	✓		✓		✓		✓		✓	Tunisia
	✓		✓	✓		✓	✓	✓		✓	Turkey
	✓	✓		✓	✓	✓	✓			✓	Uruguay
	✓	✓	✓	✓		✓	✓	✓	✓	✓	U.S.A.
	✓	✓	✓	✓		✓	✓	✓		✓	Yugoslavia
	✓			✓		✓	✓			✓	Zimbabwe

Index